Find Your Way

Find Your Way

R. K. Caroland

Visit the website at:
Zennomore.com

All rights reserved.

Copyright © 2008 by R.K. Caroland

No part of this book may be reproduced or transmitted in any form or by any means, electronic or mechanical, including photocopying, recording, or by any information storage and retrieval system, without permission in writing from the copyright holder.

This book is sold subject to the condition that it shall not, by way of trade or otherwise, be lent, re-sold, hired out, or otherwise circulated without the copyright holders prior consent in any form of binding or cover other than that in which it is published and without a similar condition including this condition being imposed on the subsequent purchaser.

Editing and design
by
Robert Zullick

ISBN: 978-0-578-02801-9

Contents

	Introduction	7
1	How it works	13
2	What it is	21
3	Differences	35
4	Value	43
5	Expectations	51
6	Authenticity	59
7	Affection	65
8	Assumptions	71

9	Manipulation	77
10	Self – Esteem	85
11	Justification	93
12	Love	97
13	Attitude	103
14	Freedom	107

Introduction

From the very beginning man has hungered for that epic journey, a trial that tests him to the very core of his being. We are a people that crave a challenge, be it physical, mental, professional or material, that search for the highest peak, the deepest ocean, or the fiercest terrain. All kinds of people seek out challenges to overcome in their lives; it is the need to understand ourselves, to find out who we really are. What is it that drives you?

You may climb Everest, explore the deepest jungles, or sail the world's oceans, but when its all over and you come down off the mountain, out of the jungle, or back from the sea, you are still faced with the same problem that you had when you began. YOU.

There are a great many challenges out there ready for the bold, but there always remains one challenge that few dare to pursue. It is not found at the peak of Everest, or at the end of a solo ocean voyage, in fact it doesn't even require a passport.

If we are searching for a challenge in our life, then we should ask why, look for the answers and follow the proof. Truly our greatest challenge is to answer the questions that we have regarding our social interactions, relationships, our place in the world and most importantly, what is the meaning of our life? OK, I'm not saying that this book answers all of our questions,

INTRODUCTION

but it does put the right questions in order to find your way towards the answer.

No one likes to ask the tough questions. The hardest thing in the world is to look at yourself and ask a question that you really don't want to know the answer to. We dodge the obvious because of what we might find out about ourselves.

It is the struggle between what we hope and dream, and denial is the obstacle of these hopes and dreams. To look at the evidence of what is really happening, and to realize the truth about our circumstances is the first step in seeing the truth. It is the old saying, if it quacks like a duck, walks like a duck, swims like a duck, more than likely it's a duck.

The trouble is between what we want the situation to be and what is truly happening. The ability to deny the true situation and create what we want is incredible. Our outer world conditioning causes us to develop psychological defense mechanisms that we use daily to compete with others. At the unconscious level, we are all driven by the need to compete with each other to prove our value and worth.

It is truly the human condition to want to be special, but when we take a moment to look at ourselves we see that we are all special. Realizing this, it then becomes our personal responsibility to try and understand ourselves better, so that the world has one less dysfunctional person. Most of us feel shame when we see our dysfunctions, but really we should see them as a challenge, and systematically conquer them.

If we do not search out every opportunity to improve our life and resolve our dysfunctions, then we are subjecting the ones we love to our inadequacies by expecting them to live with them.

FIND YOUR WAY

This shows that we do not care enough to fight our own demons, and will subject the ones we love to our terrible personal inadequacies.

Tell me, does someone who won't take on their personal inadequacies for the ones they love, truly love you? The healing of a dysfunction should take precedence over ourselves. It is the first step to selflessness, and it shows true compassion and empathy for others. It is true love for others when we try to improve ourselves for everyone involved with us. It is our personal responsibility to comprehend and resolve our personal problems, and not to expect others just to live with them.

The greatest challenge that we could ever undertake is to conquer ourselves. Once we defeat the selfishness of dysfunction, then we have defeated our greatest adversary, and nothing in this world can come close to hurting us.

This is our epic journey and the one true challenge in the world. It is the nuts and bolts of addressing the struggle with the ego, and subduing the power of the ego is a fierce battle, but a battle that can be won. Are you ready?

"To study the way is to study the self. To study the self is to forget the self. To forget the self is to be enlightened by all things."--Dogen

1

How it works

I have always been interested in how and why people react the way they do to the various situations in life. In my personal search for myself, I have learned many things about how we as people look at our lives. Researching the many sources relating to this activity has helped me understand people's reactions and how we see our environment. I have found that much of it can be traced to childhood upbringing, and social interactions.

The most surprising thing to me was the way people became addicted to their emotions and why they create this addiction. The mind's biochemical relationship to emotion, and the motivation behind self- gratification is surprising. In this book we will look at some of the triggers and the turmoil that comes with fulfilling our desires.

The human mind is a mixed bag of electrical impulses and chemicals interacting with one another to create our view of the world and of society. When we look closer at the brain's activity and how it works in conjunction to emotional responses, we can see how emotions effect the production of chemicals in our brain.

HOW IT WORKS

For example, self-gratification has remarkable effect on the human mind and body. It is that feeling of superiority that comes from winning a competition, or being the best in our field of expertise that gives us the euphoria of inflated ego esteem. This feeling originates in the brain creating endorphins and releasing them into the blood stream.

We will examine the reason behind the triggering of endorphins, the addiction to the feelings that they give us, and how this addiction to endorphins becomes a vicious cycle that is manufactured in our own mind through our own self-promotion.

Located in the human brain is the limbic system, which is involved with emotion, motivation, and memory. The limbic system is connected with a structure known as the nucleus accumbens, commonly called the brain's pleasure center. This nucleus accumbens is then connected to the prefrontal cortex.

Some scientists contend that this connection is related to the pleasure obtained from solving problems. If we can get pleasure from solving problems, then we can get pleasure from boosting our ego. When our pleasure center is activated it's always something we want, and we want all we can get, so we search for situations to get the pleasure center activated for as long and as often as possible.

The hypothalamus is the factory in the brain that makes certain chemicals, which correspond to our emotional responses from outside sources. The continuous bombardment of emotions causes the hypothalamus to create many different chemicals in the brain, anything from adrenalin to endorphins.

The hypothalamus produces endogenous opioid peptides that interact with neurotransmitters, or receptors in the brain to

FIND YOUR WAY

create anything from euphoria to pain relief. With repeated exposure to endogenous opioid peptides, more and more neurotransmitters are created in the brain. This is where the brain creates it's own craving for certain peptides.

Imagine a baseball team where we have a pitcher and a catcher, the endogenous opioid peptides are the pitchers and the neurotransmitters are the catchers. The more you crave certain emotions, the more pitchers and catchers are created.

We get addicted to having the good feelings from the ego. This is the problem with any addiction; it takes over our life and makes it painful. The release of endorphins is pleasurable and the problem with this is its addictive quality. Like any other addictive drug, it takes more and more to get that certain feeling again. People go out of their way to get this feeling and it consumes their world, disrupting relationships and happiness. This is referred to as the emotional attachment to emotion, and this book is about the consequence of the search for this kind of satisfaction.

If you were to create the perfect designer drug, I believe that the ego-esteem would be the model for that perfect drug. Our ego-esteem triggers the creation of endorphins in the brain, giving us an euphoric feeling about ourselves. It is a feeling of being important and superior to everyone else. How do you feel when you believe you are important? Or that everyone is envious of you? You get compliments about your car, house, the money you make, the street you live on, the church you go to, your job, on and on. With every complement we receive the brain releases endorphins, our drug of choice.

Since our brain releases endorphins that can be linked to the opium receptors, why would it be so surprising to see that

HOW IT WORKS

people are addicted to certain emotional responses, and will do nearly anything for that desired response. The addiction to endorphins released from emotions is the bases of ego-esteem.

What is the harm of feeling good about yourself? What does it matter that you get a euphoric feeling from self-gratification? It feels good to have these endorphins released in the brain, and the physical enjoyment of these endorphins drive many people to repeat these same actions over and over again to get these feelings. A strange thing happens when we get addicted to endorphins, we tend to seek out as many ways as possible to have these endorphins released.

Remember all the weirdness we all went through after reaching puberty? It is our normal reaction to all the new chemicals being released into our blood stream. All the hormones and testosterone that is produced at the time of puberty effects us from that point on until the day we die. Danger also elicits a chemical response. When we are faced with the option to run for our lives or stand and fight, we are reacting instinctively to what is called the acute stress response, or fight or flight, which is regulated by the sympathetic nervous system.

Some people eat or drink alcohol; others seek their comfort with drugs or sex. They are seeking these, and any number of other things most often to cover or avoid a deeper emotional problem. Take a cigarette smoker for example, they get addicted to nicotine and the more they smoke, the harder it is to change their behavior. Neurotransmitters are being hard wired to that activity, creating a new flood of peptides in the brain that causes the craving for another cigarette.

It's the same brain activity when we get attached to the feeling of certain emotions, and then search for the opportunities to create the emotional responses for physical enjoyment. People like the feeling these activities give them, so more neurotransmitters are being hardwired, and the peptides are continually being made to keep up with the demand. After a while we have pitchers and catchers almost passionately begging for more stimulation.

To believe a person doesn't receive sense stimulation from these situations, is saying that the person is disconnected from the outside world. We respond to outside influences every minute of the day, so finding the addictive qualities of endorphins and the link for the distinct yearning for attention and approval shouldn't be a surprise.

When we look at the brain and see how it works and reconfigures itself to our desires, we realize the power we have to design our own reality. Take for example anorexia. Now this is a person who has convinced him or herself that they are too heavy and actually starve themselves to death. You can't convince them of their error, because they actually see themselves totally different from the true reality, and are unable to realize that they are actually harming themselves. The power of the mind to create it's own reality for a desired affect is extraordinary.

We can create anything we want, we can make it up as we go. It doesn't matter because it's our reality. It's our own little made up world. Only denial stands as an emotional barrier to realizing this truth. It is a direct reflection of our imagined expectations, regardless of the true outcome. We don't want it to be true, so we deny its very existence.

We are taught to respond to the various life situations that we face in our culture, first by our parents, and then as we grow

HOW IT WORKS

and develop, we respond to the conditioning of the society that surrounds us. Our reactions to situations reflect the people in our society at large, and this interaction creates motives that subconsciously drive us to fulfill desires of our own making.

No one wants to ask the tough questions. The hardest thing in the world is to look at yourself and ask a question that you really don't want to know the answer to. We dodge the obvious because of what we might find out about ourselves.

It is the struggle between what we hope and dream, and denial is the protection of these hopes and dreams. To look at the evidence of what is really happening, and to realize the truth about our circumstances, is the first step in seeing the truth. It is the old saying, if it quacks like a duck, walks like a duck, swims like a duck, more than likely it's a duck.

The trouble is between what we want the situation to be and what is truly happening. The ability to deny the true situation and to create what we want is incredible. One obvious example is when our family is together, we imagine it will be pleasant because of the love we share with one another, but frequently it ends in conflict.

We struggle to understand the problems between brothers, sisters, parents and in-laws. We want everything to be joyful because we feel the kinship of family, but really most of the time there is trouble. Snide comments and personality clashes create tension for everyone. It is the underlying problem of many families because of old sibling rivalries that the parents have carried to their own marriages. The parents may have had to fight for attention as children, so they bring these old habits to the next generation.

FIND YOUR WAY

When our self-esteem depends on being right in a discussion, we will fight to the finish to be proven right because it's not the discussion that is on the line but our ego esteem. The desire for that perfect family unit quickly becomes a disappointment when personalities collide, struggling for attention and trying to protect their ego esteem. When we deny the negative, we create a false reality, an illusion rather than facing up to the way things truly are.

Denial often produces its own evidence to watch for, one example is walking around with your left arm going numb, sharp pains in your chest and telling yourself that you are not having a heart attack. All the evidence is there to support the idea that you're having a heart attack, but you believe it can't happen to you. Or, how many times has a battered woman said, "He's not a bad person just don't make him mad", or "I shouldn't have done what I did". It's the evidence of denial, and with this kind of denial of evidence, you could die.

The power of the mind to create it's own reality is amazing. The mind can be trained to do anything, so the trick is to train yourself to do what is necessary, and to understand that everything else is based on the totality of your life experiences and cultural influences. Your personal life experience creates the perception of your own reality, but keep in mind that it can be a very distorted view of life.

2

What it is

Self-esteem is how we *feel* about our *inside* qualities, our worth as human beings as *we* judge it.

Self-image is how we *think* we appear to others on the *outside*, including whether we think we are "popular," or "pretty," or "smart," based on other peoples judgments.

Ego-esteem is thinking one is (or is trying to be) *better than* others. These people feel important by making others feel unimportant and are egocentric, narcissistic and self-centered.

The need to impress other people comes from low self-esteem. It is the feeling that by ourselves we are not enough, so we live our lives trying to impress others. We try to find things that will impress others to raise what we believe is our self esteem, and once we find this particular thing outside ourselves, we begin to define ourselves with it. When we attach our ego to this "thing" we get competitive and protective about it. This is ego-esteem.

If we have built financial equity in our life, it is hard not to compare other people against our accomplishments.

WHAT IT IS

It is difficult for a wealthy person to have a close relationship with a poor person without feelings of superiority. It is human nature to compare ourselves to each other, and to evaluate ourselves by what we have achieved. There are many different ways that ego-esteem creates it's own barriers.

The appraisal of our accomplishments gives us a good feeling for what we have achieved, which relates directly to our self-confidence. When this self-confidence becomes an attitude of superiority, then the ego-esteem is involved.

When comparing ourselves to one another, we try to protect the feelings that our status has given us. It feels good to "feel" important, be it financial, intellectual, or really anything that sets us apart from others. There really isn't anything wrong about feeling good about ourselves, until our attitude becomes one of superiority.

It is difficult not to look down on others when we believe that we are superior. This attitude will be communicated by our belief of being superior because of the way we view other people. We are going to treat people in the way that we believe they rank against our own achievements. If we believe that we are smarter than the next person, then this attitude will become apparent.

How can we weigh someone else's opinion when we believe we are more intelligent than the other person? Eventually, people start to notice us devaluing their opinions, and realize that we are only looking for their agreement. This is when ego-esteem becomes the barrier to understanding, because we have decided that we are better. By not putting ourselves on a higher plateau, we can really hear others, and understand where they are coming from. Wisdom and compassion comes only to those able to listen, without judgment.

There is no quick way to understand what makes up another person's opinion, which is why taking the time to listen gives us an opportunity to formulate a coherent discussion. By discussing opinions, we get to know a person better and this helps us all to gain a greater knowledge and understanding. Truly knowing another's heart is a connection beyond wisdom.

When we compare and measure our self worth against others, it produces anxiety. This anxiety comes from the fear that someone will outdo our achievements, and make us feel inferior. This is where the ego-esteem gets in the way of life. When self-esteem becomes confused for ego-esteem, we act out in ways that we don't understand. It's the drive that forces us to react, creating the outbursts that come from nowhere, the snide belittling remarks meant to defend our fragile ego-esteem. Remarks meant to put others in their place, a put down to protect our anxiety.

With the competitive nature and anxiety that comes with ego-esteem, there is a struggle to control the center of attention. If we are around this type of a person and they demand more attention than normal, everyone else is forced to compete for attention. With all this need for attention, everyone who is in contact with this person will be deprived of attention. This is one of the reasons ego-esteem is so dysfunctional.

There has been a great deal written about the tragedies and complications of alcohol on family relationships, but when alcohol isn't present, and the children still come out of the family with the same problems, the question is why?

WHAT IT IS

Families struggling with ego esteem issues face similar problems to families with histories of alcohol abuse. There are several ways that ego-esteem presents itself in a dysfunctional family setting.

The most obvious is where there is a competition between either one or both parents and their children. Children learn to fight for attention, because of the need to be important in the family unit. When the parents compare their accomplishments to the children's achievements, the competition becomes apparent and damaging.

Ego esteem issues present themselves daily. Not just in a family setting, but also in all manner of social interactions. What people with inflated ego esteem don't understand is that they are dependent on others for their self esteem, and if there is no one around to feel superior to, then they have no one to give them their boost. This attitude of self-importance is obviously demeaning to everyone that is considered to be beneath him or her.

The need to feel important drives many people to compare and compete with everyone they know. The paradox of ego esteem is that it drives people away that don't want to compete or compare, thus leaving the alpha person without anyone to prop up their ego.

There are many different categories of bias, appearance being very big on the list of what effects people's views. For example, a person working under a car all day as a mechanic, or one who makes their living as a landscaper is often looked down upon for being dirty. Really anything can be used to live through ego esteem, being beautiful or handsome, athletic or tall.

FIND YOUR WAY

Mostly it's on the outside, and the problem with living for appearance is that it won't last forever. It does feel good to be admired for our uniqueness, but the need to impress is ego-esteem.

Secondly, we often look for our self-esteem from belongings, and tend to use these material things to compare ourselves to others, believing that other people envy us because of our life style. Many people with some level of wealth can't resist comparing themselves with the other people they come in contact with. This need to impress and identify everyone with the amount of money they make is a personal value system designed to put everyone in their proper place. By categorizing and putting others in their place, these people feel good by establishing their superiority, and it is this feeling that is so important.

Another example is education, how much or how little? Anything works as a comparative vehicle, and it is all about the competition for attention.

Once we are out to prove that we are special and above the rest, we begin to demean everyone else automatically by ranking people by our own personal value system. This idea of being special and superior runs very deep in our lives and in our society. It happens at a professional level everyday as we rate each other by our jobs and positions in society.

When an elitist attitude is part of our view of life, we tend to put up so many different prejudices, that it completely colors our view of life. A mechanic or a street sweeper usually doesn't have the same respect as a medical doctor or an airline pilot. By this value system, we rate each other everyday, and by doing so we put everyone in their proper place.

WHAT IT IS

The decision to give someone else recognition where its due, or to boost our own self worth is a very difficult decision for a person struggling with ego-esteem. It is this need for boosting ourselves with ego-esteem that makes every social situation a contest for attention. If we need the center of attention to strengthen the belief of our own self worth, then we are always looking to impress and to prove our point.

Living with ego-esteem is like living life with a chip on our shoulder, because not everyone is going to put the same value on the same things as we do, and this will make us feel that the other people around us are trying to devalue us.

One of the major problems with ego-esteem is living life through the need to impress, and if other people are not impressed, then it feels like an attack on our value. It's very hard to have a conversation with someone struggling with ego-esteem, because we may say something that conflicts with their opinion, and this will be seen as a challenge to them as a person.

Our personalizing an opinion may be seen as an affront, or disrespectful because the disagreement becomes a direct reflection of ego-esteem. This readily becomes apparent over a debate on politics, where our disagreement can be perceived as our being anything from a traitor to a communist. The bottom line is we can't disagree with someone struggling with ego esteem, without the feeling that we are betraying them and challenging their ideas.

Why is it so hard to defeat our pride and admit that we are wrong? Having to admit that we are wrong has a direct affect on ego-esteem. If we take opinions personally, then we no longer see them as an opinion. Living with ego-esteem at home or at work makes life hell, and demeans everyone else.

FIND YOUR WAY

There are many different ways ego-esteem shows itself, and each way has it's own destructive consequences, resulting in the destruction of many friendships and marriages.

Many people think that there is nothing wrong with an ego driven society, because it is what makes us get out there and make things happen in the world. However, when we look at the carnage left behind and what it has done to people, it is very difficult to defend the results of ego esteem.

The attainment of ego driven goals is how we build confidence. The drive to fulfill a goal, or a standard in our lives is not a bad thing, but it should be fulfilling enough for us to finally reach that goal, and not something to bolster our ego. If we set out to make people envious of us, then our ego has become a dysfunction. The endorphins that are released because of someone's envy is the fix that we are looking for, and not the goal of attainment. True self-esteem has nothing to do with our abilities, but of our character. We have to determine which is being questioned, our ability or our character.

If our ability to paint a picture or a house is in question, it really has nothing to do with our self-esteem. We may be a good football player, but remember that even the best players have their critics. If we take everything personally as if the game was our own, then our life ends at the end of each football season. It is a question of our ability, skill, and level of expertise that is in question, not our character.

When boosting our ego-esteem becomes the focus of our life, then we lose our direction. When our direction becomes envied for what we do or what we have, then we quit living for ourselves, and live for the desire of envy.

WHAT IT IS

There is no sense of personal growth because the only accomplishment is to gratify our self, which we eventually end up losing to our own little world. When we strive to have this gratification, then everyone else takes a back seat.

How can the ego judge it's own existence? How can ego-esteem judge self esteem when the ego makes up this esteem? This is the part of us with very little reasoning that is judging each component of the ego. We are asking our ego to provide something it does not have, reasoning. The only rationale that ego-esteem has to exist, is the desire to be envied and to get the feeling of being the center of attention. This is the subconscious mind driving us to attain more than we are, and live a life of delusion. When we live our lives through ego-esteem, we build our life on an imagined scale that only we believe, and this is the truest form of delusion. The ego has a sense of reasoning, but not true reasoning.

Our self-esteem may be the way that we define ourselves, but it's all the attachments that become our image. Ego image is the projection of what we want others to believe, not the true substance of our character. This image could be macho or feminine, rich or poor, smart or stupid, because this self-image is little more than an illusion made up of our attachments, and not the core of our character.

When we adopt an attitude of superiority in any form, it will always separate us from everyone else. When has arrogance served anyone in a positive way? The only thing it brings for sure is indifference to everyone else, and this attitude only makes us appear uncaring. How many times have we seen people who believe that they have the right to treat people any way they want? This is arrogance in full bloom, and it comes to us in many different forms.

FIND YOUR WAY

Once we believe that we are above average and special, what do people think of us? It is truly the human condition to want to be special. If we have a friend who believes that they have to be superior to everyone else, then where do we stand? If someone in a relationship believes they are superior, then someone must be below them and this automatically demeans someone.

When we build up the belief in ourselves to the point of egoism or vanity, the necessity of being special will always be the cause of trouble. Having to live with a vane person is putting up with their attitude of superiority, and this makes one person less than the other. Because of the belief that one person in the relationship is more important, they feel that it gives them the right to treat the other any way they want. When we are made to feel like a second-class citizen, then this is the ego-esteem making itself known. Vanity is egotism, and when the ego is involved anything goes.

It's our inherent need to feel special, and it is the extent of the ego that is in question, not if we are actually egoistical. For example, prejudice is ego esteem when one race believes that it's better than another, or when wealthy people believe that they are better than poor people. It's the engineer thinking that he is the only person that can design that certain bridge, or building. It's the narcissism that comes with ego, the vanity and the separation from everyone else.

Class bias is an interesting situation where we judge others by their classifications. This is discrimination by class, such as what someone does for a job, or where they were born. Discrimination from class bias, or discrimination of color of skin is the outlook of being better than another person based on superiority and vanity. This is judging other people by the color of their skin, or where and how they live.

WHAT IT IS

It is the very height of ego to believe that you are god, but many rulers of the past and even present history, have believed they were gods. There are no limits to the heights of human arrogance, and living with a person struggling with ego esteem is difficult at best, the results of their dysfunctional behavior is devastating, especially to a child in this type of family.

The paradox is that we strive to have people think that we are special when we belittle them, and this takes any significance from them because we must be right, and the battle to be right is the attachment to the ego esteem. It is the fear of appearing inept in a disagreement, or the fear of not being in control of everything and everyone, fearing what people will think of us.

When our appearance becomes the most important thing to us, substance becomes trivial. How many families look great from the outside, but are completely dysfunctional in their lives. This becomes the focus of dysfunctional families, to look great and repress the real problems in the family and their lives. This is a cycle that is replayed over and over, generation after generation, the continuing cycle of dysfunction.

A good example of a dysfunctional family is the son of proud parents, who has become a doctor, and learned from his parents to choose a good obedient wife. He has grown up watching his parents, so he goes home and demeans his wife, just like he has seen at home. He demeans her by always throwing his education in her face. The family wants to acknowledge his profession, but not his personal life. When we seek to be merged with our profession and not our personal life, we are hiding from our true selves. When we identify our life through our profession, then we don't value our identity.

FIND YOUR WAY

When our profession becomes our identity, we are hiding the ineptitude in our personal life, and this is exchanging perception for substance. Who we are as a person is much more important than what we do as a profession. Our true persona is who we are, and not what we do or have.

We base our existence on actuality, the belief of how we gauge our life, or more simply, what we believe is our reality. That which we believe becomes the attachments that we as human beings use to approximate our worth.

Here in America, we find our worth by the amount of money we make, what we do for a living and what we have in a material sense. To identify ourselves with the attachment to money, and not to our character is the reason we so often hear that money won't make us happy. It's quite true, that if we are an unhappy dysfunctional person, then money will only make us an unhappy, wealthy dysfunctional person. When the dream of riches becomes more important than our personal growth, then we are hiding from the true problem.

When we identify ourselves with our money, homes, cars and material accomplishments, then we lose our true identity and connect ourselves with the well being of these things. What would we truly rather have, money or wisdom? Which is more important, the ability to know others and ourselves, or wealth? This question is important because it tells us what we believe is important. Money will only add to the problems of a dysfunctional person, because of all the resentments and other baggage that they carry with them. Revenge might be at the top of the list, showing people that they are now important because of wealth. Wouldn't it be so much better to have wisdom and understanding first, and then allow wealth to come to us?

WHAT IT IS

Turn on any television program that has a confrontational format where people want to confront each other about their behavior. When there are two people with different opinions screaming at each other about who is disrespecting the other, then each side fights to be more important, which ends up demeaning someone. As the argument heats up, each side degenerates into repeating over and over again their opinion, never listening to what the other person is saying. Neither one gives significance to the others opinion, which truly shows disrespect. This is the dysfunction of ego-esteem, wanting to be right regardless of how they get it.

When our emotions are tied to our ego-esteem, we want people to feed our selfish needs. When our ego-esteem and our emotions are tied to the ego, we live a life of ups and downs. We feel good when we believe that everyone likes us, we feel good when we appear to be important, we feel good when we think other people envy us, and we feel good when other people look up to us. But what happens when people don't like us or we are not important to them, or envy us or look up to us? What happens then to our self-esteem?

This is all based on outside approval and not everyone is going to do these things for us. This is what happens when we confuse emotional ties to our ego-esteem. Our emotional tie to feeling like a big shot creates the endorphin rush, but it has nothing to do with real feelings. How many times have we heard someone brag about what they do for a living, just to find out later that they made it out to be more than it was? The need to stand out and be someone important is a major driving force in the hunger for ego-esteem.

Another indicator of ego esteem is that we hate it when someone makes fun of us. If we can't laugh at ourselves for doing something funny, then the ego esteem is involved.

FIND YOUR WAY

How can we joke with someone when their ego-esteem is their identity? When we make a joke about them, they see us as making them a joke. We are not going to be funny to this person, because it is a criticism to their personal image, and the joke is going to be perceived as an attack. How can we relax when our life is judged by our attachments and our importance?

The paradox of ego esteem is trying to find fulfillment through the attachment to false feelings, brought on by the superiority ranking of our own making, that doesn't really exist. Because it is all a figment of our own imagined importance, it is what we choose to believe that is important, or our own agendas. We are judging the world through our own ranking system against what we believe is important. Not everyone is going to agree with what we believe is important, thus making anything we judge our life against as useless. We have created our own living hell, by being judged against what we believe as important, and what doesn't really exist.

3

Differences

It is important for us to understand that self-esteem has nothing to do with any outside persuasion, whereas ego esteem is completely supported by it. The following are some of the differences between self-esteem and ego esteem.

Self-esteem is based mostly on character and virtues, whereas ego esteem is formed often at the expense of others in order to get an endorphin rush, which makes us feel good. The biggest question about the ego-esteem and self-esteem is what are we willing to sacrifice to keep them. Would we sacrifice our family? Would we sacrifice our friends? Would we sacrifice our life? It's just a question of how far people are willing to go to protect their ego-esteem and self esteem.

We must be careful where we get our value, because we may be giving away something that we never intend to.

Self-esteem is based on what is admirable about us. Our integrity, honesty, goodness, trustworthiness and humility form the elementary qualities that shape healthy self-esteem. It makes us feel good for the right reasons when we are admired for being authentic and true to our inherent nature.

DIFFERENCES

To have healthy self-esteem, we should be self-contained, looking for no outside support, which is the essence of _self_-esteem. A sure way to protect our self-esteem is to make sure that we make ethical decisions based on the qualities mentioned above.

We all make choices concerning our character everyday. This is one of the first steps in realizing what is essential in life, our healthy self-esteem and coping skills. One great boost to our personal self-esteem is knowing that people can depend on us. It really helps to build our self-esteem when we are trustworthy and can be taken on our word. When all doubt about our reliability can be erased, we then can be a person that others can put confidence in. Trust is truly a valuable commodity in the world today, much more even than gold.

Having true self-esteem is the hardest thing in the world, because standing up for what we believe against peer pressure takes colossal strength. We should always base our self-esteem on truth, regardless of the consequences to the ego. Fighting the power of the ego is a fierce battle, but a battle that can be won. It may not be easy at first, but most things that lead to a greater experience in life rarely are. When we base our self-esteem on truth, we live a life in true reality. It is important for us to understand that we must be honest with ourselves, and with others to truly live a life of freedom.

We should ask ourselves again, how important are my friends and family to me? What would I do to keep them as my friends, or to stay on their good side? How far would we go for approval from our friends or our family? This may seem like a strange question, but the reason will soon become apparent.

FIND YOUR WAY

We want people to like and respect us for being compassionate and caring. So we try not to say things to others that may hurt their feelings. We often shy away from an unpleasant confrontation instead of dealing with a behavior problem.

In this time of political correctness, we don't want people to think that we are uncaring and thoughtless. This attitude is living a life for approval-esteem of others, regardless of the consequences.

Would we let our friends drive drunk, if it meant that we wouldn't have an argument? How many people have lost friends in drunk driving accidents because they didn't want to make them mad? How many things do we let people do that we don't like, and not speak up so that they don't get mad at us?

If some friends are doing drugs, do we join them just because we seek their approval, or do we do what we believe is right? If we give in to peer pressure, then we are feeding our approval needs. If we can't think for ourselves and do what we believe is right, then we deny ourselves. When we feel the peer pressure to do something that we are not comfortable with, then we are selling our esteem for another's approval. Here lies the paradox, by following the group for approval, we give away what we believe is right. If we don't do what our group wants us to do then we will lose their approval, but if we do give in, we lose ourselves. When we understand what drives our decision-making, we will not be disappointed with the results, because we have chosen our own path. It is really up to us to pick our path in life.

It's all about what we truly believe is the right thing to do, and not what we do to seek approval. All of our decisions have a price, one path we have no choice because we seek everyone's approval, and the other is our life by our own choice.

DIFFERENCES

This approval-esteem destroys our self-esteem because we can't be everything to everyone, so satisfying our need for approval esteem leads us to look for that approval from everyone, which makes this path frustrating and unfulfilling.

If our parents want us to have a career that we absolutely hate, do we do it anyway to gain their approval? Many children believe that they can get their parents approval by doing what is expected of them, regardless of the consequences to their own feelings. When we start ignoring our own emotional beliefs and do what our parents or others expect of us, we lose sight of our emotional compass. We must be true to ourselves and do what we think is right. When we live with a good sense of self-esteem, we have the strength to live with the disappointment of others.

To seek approval-esteem gives us an excuse for our behavior, and subjects us to a lot of conduct from others that we wouldn't normally endure. An example of this is the enabler in a co-dependent relationship that gets the release of endorphins of ego esteem, because the person that they're helping needs them. They get their boost through the approval of another person who is in need. The enabler will give as many excuses as the other person needs to condone their behavior because they want to be liked and needed. Thus becoming the most important person to the dysfunctional persons life.

Each person feeds off the other's approval, and condones one another's behavior. It feels good to be needed, to be important in another's life. So we enable the person to continue their destructive behavior, and we live with this dysfunctional personality. We have to manage all the unfounded feelings and fears that come with a co-dependent relationship.

FIND YOUR WAY

Living with a dysfunctional person, and taking care of all their feelings and fears becomes very taxing, but this is the price we pay to be important to the co-dependent person. Most of us try to get along in life, trying not to hurt other peoples feelings, but sometimes we let people get away with unhealthy behavior just for their approval, selling our self esteem for approval esteem.

One of the common excuses we hear right after someone subjects another to unhealthy behavior is, "Oh he really didn't mean what he said, if you get to know him, he's really a good guy." These types of excuses open the door to any kind of behavior. When seeking this person's approval, we reinforce their right to act in a socially unacceptable way, and our excuses only strengthen their right to this type of behavior.

This type of behavior is often seen with couples, in which one of them is the wild one, and the other is the voice of reason that spends their time smoothing over the ruffled feathers of others. This is the very definition of co-dependence. Much of this has been written about before, but they often don't explain the mechanics of what we are doing to ourselves and to the others around us.

Co-dependants are showing the world their real personality, but they are sure to treat the enabler better than others, because they want the enabler to approve of them. The real reason they like us, is because we give them the excuse they need to feel good about themselves. There are so many different kinds of destructive behavior, that it truly seems harmless until we realize the consequences of losing our self-esteem and suppressing our emotions for approval.

DIFFERENCES

Here is an example, when in the heat of argument we can't remember the things we want to say just then, so we think that we are no good at expressing ourselves making us feel that it's useless to even try. The reason we can't express ourselves is because of our suppressed emotions. One voice in our head is saying, "I shouldn't be treated this way", and another voice is saying, "I don't want to make this person dislike me". We are suppressing and pushing down these emotions all at the same time, so very little can be expressed without the fear of disapproval.

What are we protecting our approval-esteem, or our self-esteem? The more we deny our emotional feelings about how we are being treated, the more we suppress those emotions into something that can't ever be expressed because of the fear of disapproval.

Just remember, that we should know our true feelings, and not confuse them with ego-esteem. When our emotions are tied to our ego-esteem, we want people to feed our needs, and one of our needs is for approval, the other is to be all things to all people. This tug of war between the need for approval and the need to stand up for our true self-esteem is the root of understanding our true self.

Its often much easier to just roll with the punches than to throw them back, but we are only letting the unacceptable behavior continue by enabling it. If we don't complain or fight back, then it's perceived as if we condone this type of behavior. This is one of the many reason people act out with bad behavior, because somebody is encouraging them, either by not saying anything, or by giving them an excuse for the behavior.

FIND YOUR WAY

Here's an example of an excuse we might hear from our mother about our father after he has yelled at us. "He treats you this way because he is under tremendous pressure at work." So he is encouraged to continue this behavior as he sees fit. Usually this behavior stems from some anger issues that don't even have anything to do with us. Sometimes it's because he can't complain to his boss, or someone he works with because of the consequences it might bring. So he bottles up his frustration and it spills out at his family.

When we are frustrated and can't seem to find a way of expressing it, it usually finds an outlet in anger. There are so many things in the world that can frustrate our parents, and often none of these things is our fault.

It is a very hard lesson for us to realize that we will have to question every bad situation in our lives, just to see if we are standing up for ourselves. Self-esteem is something we know about ourselves to be true, something important we stand for.

4

Value

Some of the biggest questions in life are; why do we do the things that we do, and having done them, why can't we control our actions. It is the subconscious desires of the mind that motivate us to want the things that we want, and do what we do. It is the subtle almost invisible drive that takes place within us, and often leaves us not knowing why things turn out the way they do. The impulse response to feed our need to feel valued, leads us to respond without thinking. Let's find out where this need to feel valued started.

The first place we look to find our values is from within our family, the origin or beginning of our self-esteem. Our role and place in life is set through the influence of our early family life, stemming from how much significance they place on us. When we were growing up, if we were treated as a significant person in the family, then we should gain significance in life, however if we were treated as if we were insignificant and a burden, we will believe it.

If we are belittled and made to feel inferior, then this is what we will carry with us throughout our life. When we don't find value in our family unit, we try to find it anywhere and everywhere that

VALUE

we can. Trying to find our self-esteem within a family that doesn't value us is impossible.

This is where the subconscious desire for value becomes a lifelong search for value and self esteem. If these subconscious problems are never acknowledged, we can't grow emotionally because we get stuck right at that place of need, and are unable to move forward. Because of our dysfunctional childhood, we are carrying this need to feel valued, and as an adult, we become stuck in the past. Regrets and bitterness about the past will never make the present change, and by resenting our past, we live in what was, and not what is, the now. It is very hard for us to learn what we really need to feel good about ourselves, if we didn't have the proper guidance as a child.

The subconscious desire to defend our value comes from low self-esteem. We often find people trying to prove themselves to their family, friends, or the people around them in many ways. This behavior is brought forward from the past, stemming from that point in time that they felt inferior in some way, which causes them to try and prove their value and importance.

This subconscious drive to prove ourselves is driven by the desire to gain stature. This drive to gain stature can show up in many different places, because it has now become a trigger that will set us off whenever we feel inferior. We want to hide our insecurity from everyone, and usually do it by lashing out to defend our dysfunction. So in essence, everyone ends up paying for our insecurity.

Our subconscious desire for value will lead us to fulfill our need in surprising ways. If our ego has to be stroked, we will be drawn to a person that will fill that particular desire.

FIND YOUR WAY

This creates our own little security zone around us, and once we have created our own little support group, we can have every desire fulfilled because the enabler's job is to be our emotional stability.

Through our insecurity we feel victimized, and like everyone is out to insult us because of our attachment to being the boss. Being an alpha personality, we must always be in control, and if we are not someone is out to harm us. It is the attachment of always getting our way, and if we are challenged for control, we lash out because of the insecurity of not being in control.

The fear of not being the most important person will lead us into a meltdown, which is where our carefully constructed security zone comes into play. This support group knows what is expected, and tolerates the behavior of the dysfunction. This subconscious desire leads to a family unit that is closed off from everyone else, and has to adhere to its particular families rules. This creates children that can't cope in the outside world without guidance. The children go back to their families for advice for nearly everything, and this becomes the disabling effects of dysfunction.

The children were never given the opportunity to decide anything for themselves, because the alpha personality had always been in charge of everything in their lives. The alpha personality thought they knew best for everyone involved, which gave them their value. These rules are the security zone that the alpha personality must have around them to protect their own insecurities.

Remember, if your family is dysfunctional, the alpha person has found the people to protect their insecurities. So the family members know to relent to the alpha person and not to question

VALUE

the rules of the house, because this is questioning the importance of the alpha person. If someone outside of the family questions the rule, the co-dependents will come to the aid of each other, and that's the security system that was set up for the protection of the alpha person.

One person protecting the esteem of the other, this is the role of a co-dependent. The alpha personality will demand most of the attention of the family. As children of an alpha personality, one of the subconscious desires that usually manifest itself is the craving for attention to validate something that will make them feel valuable. In this search to be valuable, we yearn to find someone or something that will fill the hole of not being valued. This subconscious desire will lead us in many different confusing directions and situations, just so we can find our self worth. But always remember, healthy self worth means finding value from within.

The subconscious desire for value drives us to find someone that understands us, and will give us value. It feels good when someone gives us praise, and this is enough attraction for some people. This kind of attraction to each other is thought of as a good thing, when it's only an attraction to fulfill neediness. Here comes a slippery slope. If the attraction is from some search of value rather than some form of admiration for the person, then we are basing our love on fulfilling a need rather than respect and admiration.

The demeanor of a person with low self esteem, his or her reactions of anxiety, the feeling of being uncomfortable around others, the feeling of not believing in ourselves and finally, the lack of self confidence, is all broadcast to the world. This demeanor of dysfunction is the lure of attraction to another dysfunctional person.

FIND YOUR WAY

Other people suffering from dysfunction understand these reactions of dysfunction, and the attraction is felt. This attraction serves as a way for us to fulfill each other's needs for self value from someone else.

We obtain this self-value from helping the dysfunctional partner cope with the world. This comes from the feeling that we understand each other and feel that a connection has been made. Unfortunately, what we don't understand is that this is the first step in enabling each other to hide from the world.

The definition of dysfunction is an "abnormal or impaired functioning, especially of a bodily system or social group." I think it's very important to define dysfunction, because there are so many of us in this world that don't know what being dysfunctional actually is.

When we go out to search for someone to fulfill us, we are asking this person to take on everything that we won't confront ourselves. This is too much to ask of any person other than ourselves. The need to be important in the relationship pushes us to demand as much attention as we can get from our partner.

The attraction to fulfill a dysfunction for someone else is itself an illness. The resulting attraction then becomes an unhealthy relationship, dominated by struggle through the demands of who will be fulfilled by the other. We then begin to realize that our relationship has become a burden to endure, nothing more than an exercise in fulfilling each other's dysfunction. This struggle for value becomes a never-ending contest for fulfillment.

After this dysfunctional relationship fails, we have trouble understanding why we can't find that perfect person. Each time we tell ourselves this person is different, but our dysfunction

VALUE

guarantees us the same results. This is the reason many children of alcoholics end up marrying an alcoholic, because of the attraction of the dysfunction. We can never understand why someone would knowingly marry an alcoholic, when we know the heartbreak of these relationships. But, then this is normal behavior to some, because it is how they grew up. When we are raised in a home of extremes, how can we be expected to know what is not normal?

When we are subconsciously drawn to people by trying to fulfill a need, it becomes dependence on another person. The need for someone else to complete us is relying on the other person to fulfill our personal flaws. This is putting a great deal of pressure on the other person who we are depending on to fulfill us, when they may have enough trouble of their own.

The subconscious desire to feel good about ourselves can lead us to believe co-dependent behavior is beneficial to both of us in the relationship. When we see each other in the relationship as crutches, we are not functioning as a whole person. We are actually asking the other person to participate in an incomplete or half of a relationship, because we are not all there to participate. The need to fill the hole in our life is a very powerful hunger, and most people will find someone or something to fill it with, at least temporarily.

This relationship becomes a stifling drain on our partner. The demands of time and energy are overwhelming because of the anxiety we have in our life. Since we are not able to maintain our own emotional stability, we depend on our partner for stability. This is an unhealthy relationship that we have all seen, where the people in this type of relationship are unable to function on their own. We can't let the other person out of our sight, because we feel threatened and vulnerable due to our low self-esteem.

FIND YOUR WAY

When we feel the need to be someone else's security blanket to protect their dysfunction, then we ourselves are dysfunctional.

If we are drawn to people who need help in their lives, then this is the basis for co-dependent behavior. If we are helping someone in his or her life, this gives us the feeling of being important, which gives us our value. This subconscious motivation for value has us jumping from one of our partners' problems to another, and fixing our own all at the same time. Then we wonder why the relationship is so taxing.

The insecurities of a co-dependent demands constant reassurance, once the benchmark of love becomes the enabling of a dysfunction, we find that it is the importance we gain by enabling them to hurt themselves. The benchmark is that we are taking care of them, and this shows that we love them.

We can't understand why it's wrong to enable them when it makes us feel good for taking care of them, and that the enabled person is not hurt mentally or physically. When we have to be the buffer in life for someone who can't exist without help, then we are adding to the emotional baggage of the enabled.

This type of behavior is fulfilling the need to feel valued. One example is, "I'm his mother and I'm going to keep my child from being hurt". Who is gaining importance here, the mother or the child? Is she important by being the protector and showing that she loves her child, or is she condemning her child to a lifetime of pain in the real world?

Once this child grows up and leaves his mothers protection to become the person he was meant to be, who is going to be there to protect him, since he never learned to do it himself?

VALUE

This is where self-confidence and self-esteem is destroyed in the name of love. There are many parents who don't understand that it is the world that gives us strength, and healthy self-esteem. If we hide from the real world, we are condemned to live in a world of our own making.

Some of us must have other people in our own little world that can protect us from everyone else in the real world. It is like a person that can't stop doing drugs because of some pain in their life. What is going to happen? What always happens in these situations? What about the person that can't relate to the world, and can't find the esteem to live their life without their own personal hell? Where is the caring and love found when we continue to be the buffer, the strong one in the relationship?

All we are doing is keeping them in their own personal hell. Where is the love? It is the parent that knows at some point that they must let their children find their own way in the world, and gain the confidence to live life.

True love is letting people gain confidence to live a fruitful life. It is the gaining and the progress toward a happier life that is important. In a codependent relationship there is no progress, no gaining, just being stuck in a personal hell of our own making. No one ever said it would be easy to let the people we love make mistakes and have pain in their lives, but at some time or another, we all must learn to stand up for ourselves. It is the person that won't let us learn to cope in the world that truly doesn't love us. If someone wants to shield us from the world and do everything for us so we won't have pain, then this only ensures our failure in real life. This is not caring for someone; this is injuring and obstructing the healthy development of the person.

5

Expectations

How much of our life is governed by the expectations of others? One of the subconscious desires that motivate us to do things is from the need to please others. Trying to live up to everyone else's expectations of us is very difficult, if not impossible. In the case of a family, the problem with expectations is that the children tend to become a reflection of the parents. All children seek the approval of their parents, and some parents use this need to manipulate and live vicariously through their children, be it in sports, occupations or whatever the child is doing. This puts a tremendous amount of pressure on the child to validate their parents, and in the end the child ends up living for the family instead of for his or herself.

A good example might be, would a doctor be proud of his or her child if they become a mechanic, or if the daughter married one? Why, because this reflects back directly on the parents and their ability to raise their children. It's not a question about whether the child enjoys being a mechanic or is deeply in love with someone who is, it's a question of how it looks to the family. The well being of the child takes a back seat to what is perceived to be important, namely the family status.

EXPECTATIONS

In this example we face the danger of losing our individual identity within the family, because whatever we do is a reflection on the family. If I speak my mind, I'm speaking for myself and not for the entire family. It is difficult for a parent to sit back and not interfere in the life of their children as they decide on their future.

If we lose sight of the real reason we choose our own occupation, then we may get trapped in a life we hate. If we work just for the money and not for the pleasure the job gives us, then not only does our work suffer, but so does the quality of our lives. How do you do a good job at something you hate? Find something that you love, and make a living doing it without worrying about the money or the prestige. Some of the most successful people will tell you that's how they did it.

How can we be ourselves while living up to other people's expectations? When we bend to the expectations and desires of our families or others, we have a difficult time understanding why we feel so empty. Are we living our own life or someone else's?

How can we expect to find fulfillment living up to the expectations of those who aren't fulfilled themselves? Their dependence creates our dependence; their characteristics become our characteristics, so continues the cycle of our lives, dependence upon dependence. This continues until we choose to no longer be trapped in this behavior, and stop letting people manipulate us into these unending cycles. How can we concentrate on our own life, when everyone else expects so much from us?

It's a razor's edge to walk between what is good for someone we care about, and what's good for us, keeping in mind that not

FIND YOUR WAY

all expectations are bad, but we must understand the motivation behind the expectations. Looking for value solely through what our parents, grandparents or friends consider important is difficult, although worth considering as advice and options to our own choices.

Let me offer you a little history of my grandfather, and invite you to see from his prospective. Born in Tennessee in the eighteen nineties, he learned to hunt and fish for survival as a youth. Then in the early nineteen hundreds the family decided to move west to Oklahoma. He accompanied them by walking behind the families' wagon the entire way. These stout people were the pioneers of an early Oklahoma homestead. My grandfather's life was filled with the importance of cutting out a place in the Wild West. He grew up in a time when men were the protectors of what they owned and who they loved.

This was how he lived, and it shaped his perspective on what a man grew up to be. How can anyone expect to measure up to this type of life in this day and age? Measured against this rigid perspective, I would never be a man. Growing up in the fifties, my life looked very easy and soft to him. I know it sounds very strange, until you realize that at the time of his childhood, it was a fight to stay alive from the elements, and finding enough food to eat on the frontier. All he wanted was for me to grow up and be a man, the only problem was his perspective was shaped in a time that no longer existed.

He told me of a great flood that devastated the area in 1919, and how life was hard and rewarding on the frontier. He told me of a time when he was making extra money working on the roof of a building in a nearby town, and watched as two men had a shoot out over a woman in the middle of the street. These were two of his examples of saying you take care of your own.

EXPECTATIONS

My grandfather loved me in his own strange way and tried to make me into the man he thought I should be. When I was ten, a friend of my grandfather who was born in eighteen seventy two, told me the story of how his father had a shoot out with some Indians that were trying to steal their horses. Life becomes a time capsule forming our perceptions of life, and my grandfather formed his by a full lifetime of events, such as world war one and two, the economic depression, and of course his life on the frontier.

Expectations often turn into a personal history lesson because we gauge what's important, and bring it into the time that we are living. This is one of the many problems with trying to live up to others people's expectations. My grandfathers rigid expectations could have driven me to do many things I normally would not do, in an attempt to try and impress him. How was I to live up to the expectations of my grandfather's particular life experience? How could I have possibly related to his experiences of becoming a man, in this day and age?

My parents grew up in the economic depression of the nineteen twenties, and because of this experience money is important. My grandparents grew up on the homestead, where survival on a new frontier was important.

So using my life as an example, how could I apply and shape my life in this day and age using the standards, expectations and values of my father and grandfather? I took what I could use from my upbringing, and set out to find my own way in life, without trying to prove anything to anybody. In this way I found what was best for me, and in the process, I found out who I am.

FIND YOUR WAY

Expectations can often lead to resentments. When parents have resentment against their children, who they believe have had it easier, life becomes a paradox. Parents strive to give their children a better life than they had growing up, but in doing so many parents feel that their children don't appreciate the opportunity.

The paradox is in striving to give our children a better life, then to think that they are taking it for granted, and that they believe they deserve the opportunities without striving on their own. They resent the belief that they had to work for everything, and the children had it handed to them.

Every generation thinks the same thing about the next generation. Our parents heard the same resentments as they grew up. How many times did our parents hear that they had it so easy, followed by the old tale of walking ten miles to school, barefoot in the snow? If we believe that we had to struggle to get what we have, then we resent what we think was easier to receive.

Is it our parents fault that they were born in a time when public schools had school buses? Is it our fault that our parents struggled to give us a better life? The problem is in the resentment that we got it too easy, becoming once again a history problem. In the past things were different, past generation's see that this generation is having it easier, but it's not our fault. If we minimize someone's achievements because we think that they have it easier, we are demeaning them.

A good example is in this time of prosperity, there comes a certain expectation of prosperous parents paying for their children's higher education. Living up to these expectations of parents paying for a college education is a burden.

EXPECTATIONS

The expectations of being prosperous and of upholding this image for their self value, their ego-esteem is in direct conflict with giving to someone they believe has had it too easy. This is the paradox.

No one has asked to be born into a prosperous family; it's not the child's fault. It's also not the child's fault that their parents were born in a different time, where college and everything else was less expensive. It's not the child's fault that there is a resentment of what is perceived as the easier life. It's not the parent's fault that their parents thought the same thing.

It is the fault of the parents that creates this resentment, because they want to appear to be able to afford to send their children to college and pay for it, but they feel that they are taken for granted. This is the way that some parents gain their ego-esteem, by seeking respect from their parents, especially if they didn't pay for their college. So in the end, we are living with parents that think that everything was handed to us on a silver platter, because we didn't do what they did to go to college.

All this is like being mad at our kids because computers were invented, thus making their schoolwork easier, or our grandparents getting mad at our parents because they didn't have to walk to school in the snow, because cars were invented. So essentially, every generation has had it easier than the one before. This is called progress, and isn't that why we go to college?

When I was growing up, my father didn't know what a computer was, and my grandfather couldn't even understand what it did. To our generation the computer is a common tool in our lives, used for virtually everything from school to business and everything in between.

FIND YOUR WAY

So, if I had become a successful computer engineer, what would my parents and grandparents think? It's not from their time, so how could it be relevant?

Now let's throw a different culture into the mix, which has the additional cultural expectation, as well as expectations from parents and grandparents. The cultural background may come from the old country, be it Sweden, Japan or India. How would you like to be expected to live up to these expectations in another time and culture?

Times have changed to where comparing our lives with our parents or grandparents is nearly impossible. But we still have these subconscious desires and cravings to fulfill the dreams of others. When our self-esteem is connected to others through expectations, we will never find happiness. Our parents might say, "We're a little disappointed that you didn't become the doctor we wanted you to be." This way they are making sure that the behavior of living through someone else will never change, because someone will always validate this behavior, thus insuring that it will never change. Expectations have a way of sucking the joy out of life.

6

Authenticity

Who of us wants to have a confrontation in our life? Who wants to argue and fight? What good does it do? We understand that we really don't want to hurt other people's feelings; we don't want to look like we are not caring, we do care about other people's feelings. All we really want is to have people like us. What does it hurt? How can we criticize someone for trying to find his or her importance and value in life? So, as politely as we can, we go about our lives.

Everyone knows someone who has that classic alpha personality, who likes to brag on what they have or what they've done. This bravado typically includes a bossy attitude, and this attitude demands everyone who is around this person to be submissive. If we are not submissive, the alpha sees this as a challenge to their influence to the group or family. They like to be in control of the group, and decide what the group will do. The bossy types get mad if we don't let them have control, so we let them direct the group of friends or family in whatever they want to do. What does it hurt?

If we have to give up our self-direction for someone else's insecurities, then we are giving up too much. It is the control of an individual or group that gives this type of person value.

AUTHENTICITY

Being in control is the only way they know to have assurance of their value. If we are letting someone control us into a direction that they are sure is right for us, then we have given up our right to decide for ourselves.

There are many people in this world that think they know what's best for us, much better than we do. How much are we going to give up just to get along and to please everyone? How much are we willing to tolerate? How far are we willing to go to have friends, and have people like us? I have personally known people that let their friends be seriously hurt, because they were afraid of the consequences of saying something. This is the fear of disapproval.

People pleasers get their value by their popularity, and living through this popularity makes them seek the approval of friends and family. Saying yes to anyone that asks something of us because at that moment, the people pleaser inside us is getting value. "I'm a good person and people like me"," I'm valued".

To live our life as a popularity contest in order to find out what we believe about our self is a self-esteem issue. By doing this, how much of ourselves are we sacrificing? What harm will this do?

If we feel that we have to agree with everyone to be accepted, our authenticity is sold. Our ability to be genuine and authentic is gone. We will sell our true self-esteem for approval. When we focus on approval, we become a chameleon and change to fit everyone, so that we will have that person's approval.

It's a form of control of perception; if we are perceived as a helpful caring person then we are valued. With careful manipulation, we can get what we desire, popularity.

FIND YOUR WAY

By seeking this approval we enable all kinds of behavior, and provide excuses for our friends or family such as never saying anything that is unpleasant or, what they didn't want to hear, or something that might embarrass them. No criticisms because the approval of our friends and family is more important than what we truly believe for ourselves.

Here is the paradox. In one way we have friends, but we can't have our own self-esteem because that rests on our friends approval. If our life is lived for other peoples approval, then what about our dignity? Do we sell our dignity for approval?

When we manipulate other people's feelings by saying what we know they want to hear, we sell out our authenticity. Can we then be trusted to say what we truly believe, or are we afraid to be ourselves at the cost of losing a friend? No one knows if we are telling the truth, or just saying what we think everyone else wants to hear. Where is the authenticity? In manipulating other people's feelings, we are not saying what we really believe and are basing our friendships on dishonesty.

It is the greatest paradox of the people pleaser. In not saying what we believe, we can't have self-respect. This becomes the hole we can't fill. This is why we have the feeling that we are not valued and are constantly seeking something we can believe in. How can we feel fulfilled, when we are hiding what we truly believe? This becomes the hole in ourselves, when we deny our own truth. If we are not truthful about what we really think, then how in the world can we find something to believe in? If we know we are lying for approval, how can we ever be believed, and how can being dishonest give us self-esteem?

AUTHENTICITY

When our self-esteem is based on being dishonest for the sake of being popular, then this becomes a hole in our soul, a great big hole that we can't find a way to fill. Being driven by the subconscious desire for approval to prove our importance from person to person leaves us little time to make room for our lives.

This is why we have friends that are always late, and we know if we say anything about them being late, it will hurt their feelings or make them mad. So to keep our friend happy, we don't say anything. Our friend is just always late. We have been late for movies, or have completely lost out on some activities, because we had to wait for our friend. When the people pleaser is getting attention and approval, he or she will stay as long as they can, because through this comes their value and a feeling of importance.

It is very hard for this person to leave, because of the feeling of importance to the person in front of him at this time. So the time flies and they know we will let them get away with making us wait. He or she knows we will let them get away with this behavior because we are a people pleaser too. It's been proven that one of the reasons that people make us wait, is that it makes them feel important because we are waiting for them.

Here is another example, we know people that must have all their friends meet up and have a meal together, but in getting everyone together it turns into a waiting game on one person or another, until finally everyone manages to get together. It can be hours waiting for everyone's schedule to come together, but why is it so important for everyone to eat together? How does it make us feel when all of our friends are around us, and sharing the companionship we have with them?

FIND YOUR WAY

Remember those chemicals in the brain that are released through outside stimuli? It feels good to have this party of friends because this gives some people a rush of endorphins, a high. Some people relate this as value, importance and their approval esteem, so what's the harm? We let our friends get away with behavior like this because we want them to like us. Living for popularity is like a politician that can't stand up for anything. This politician flip-flops from one opinion to another, until he or she feels the majority agrees with them. This is a hole that we feel in our life because we don't stand up for anything.

The cost of our real true persona is to high a price for anyone to pay for mere popularity. How can any person truly know us if we are not showing who we really are? If we are not sharing what we are really thinking, then we are living a deception and denying our true feelings. What kind of weird mind clash comes from this? How can we know if we are coming or going? Does anyone have to ask why we feel lost or confused in life?

Another paradox comes after we realize people are doing the same thing to us by manipulating our feelings and telling us what we want to hear. Just put yourself into their position, and realize that they would say anything to make us feel better. Life now becomes a place where we know that what everyone is saying does not mean anything.

We now have nothing to hold on to that is real and trustworthy. This is the reason why we can't feel better when our friends or family tell us that we are a good person, because subconsciously we are thinking that they are just trying to make us feel better. When we question the motive behind the praise, then we begin to question what our friends are telling us. We know they don't want to hurt our feelings. So here again is the great big hole that can't be filled.

AUTHENTICITY

If we are in an enabling relationship then we are not going to hear the truth, but only what the enabler thinks we want to hear. The enabler is trying to keep us from feeling unhappy. If we are the type of person that manipulates others, then most likely our friends manipulate our feelings as well, and without grounding in what is real, we are putting a smiling face on a dead body.

It is difficult to disagree with anyone because it might look bad on us. If it's true what we say to them to make them feel better, then it's not a problem. But if we manipulate feelings to validate someone just so they can feel good, then it's a lie.

The people pleasers mind races every time one of his or her friends are around. They are driven to make as many friends as they can. This person juggles his self worth with the amount of friends he believes he has.

People pleasers live with what I call the ten thousand voices. They worry how people perceive them. "Did I say the right thing"? They worry if someone is mad at them. They worry what people are thinking about them. They worry if someone thinks badly of them. They worry how everyone feels, if everyone is happy. They are always asking you if everything is okay. He or she worries if they are happy. If someone is mad at them, it will hurt what they believe is their self-esteem. I have no problem with people wanting to make other people feel good about themselves, until they are not being real. Our true self worth is much to valuable to lose, just for shallow approval and empty popularity.

7

Affection

Everyone would like to put love and caring in a box, so that we would have a simple and easy way to show that we care. When we search for proof of this intangible thing, we tend to put our own standards on it. If you care for me you will send me flowers on my birthday, or remember a special day of the month, or maybe even cook a surprise meal. However, if you don't fit into my perspective of love or friendship, then you are neither friend nor lover. It's the proof that is important, something concrete to show for it.

There was a teenager from a broken home that grew up with his mother. He told me that his father didn't love him because he couldn't remember his birthday. I personally knew his father quite well, and I recall that right after the child's birth, wherever the father went the child was there with him, in fact they were inseparable. This boy's father was, and still is a very macho kind of guy, so when he began to carry the infant everywhere he went we were all very surprised.

This child was never deprived of anything, because he was the very center of his father's world. This behavior became very difficult for everyone who spent any time around the father and son, because if the boy wanted to do something, we all did what

AFFECTION

the kid wanted. In fact, this was the main reason I stopped going on vacations with them. We all understand that it's important to show a child that we care for them, and in this case his father did everything he could, and here was the boy now a teenager, facing a crisis.

What did this man have to do to prove he cares for his son? I took this teenager aside, and asked him if he remembered anything that he had done with his father. I explained to him, that people spend their lives searching for someone who will have their back when things go wrong. Sadly, the relationship between the father and son changed after the mother took the boy and moved clear across the country after a nasty divorce.

It was amazing to see all of the things the father did and sacrificed for his child, and then the child declared it's not enough. This causes us to see that if we get everything, then nothing means anything. When we expect everything, then how can anything be enough? Looking back, I could not think of anything that this child didn't get when he wanted it. If our every whim and desire is given to us, then how could we possibly appreciate it? There would be no reason for our appreciation, because we would never have been denied anything.

True appreciation comes from the understanding of relativity. Only by experiencing a lack of something, can we truly appreciate someone changing his or her mind, so that we can have what we want. If there had been something that the child had been denied, then he would have learned to appreciate what he received. If we know that we will always get our way, then how could we possibly appreciate anything?

Now in this case, the mother may have encouraged the sons attitude about his father by throwing away the birthday cards, or

FIND YOUR WAY

lied to the father when he called, planting the seeds of doubt in the boys mind. Whatever the case, the boy forgot about all that the father had done in the past, and things where not as they seemed to this teen. When we put our own expectations and perspectives on a desired result, if they are not met then you don't love me.

In my family it was the relationship with my grandfather that caused me to question and search for the many different things that create the mix of perspectives of love. As a child, my grandfather would give me unusual Christmas gifts, not the kind of gifts you would normally give a boy. On Christmas morning I would excitedly tear open my presents, and find that he would have given me baking flower and a sifter, telling me to go bake a cake.

As a seven or eight year old boy, this was the most insulting thing in the world! Well I would run to my mother and cry, and she would comfort me, and of course my grandfather would see this as coddling and babying me. He would complain to her that she shouldn't protect me so much, and that next year he was going to buy me a dress.

My mother wouldn't really say much back to my grandfather, this was the fifties, and you just didn't do that. Your elders always knew better, and you sure didn't argue. Now, on the other hand was my grandmother, and every time he would pull something like that, she would jump in there and let him have it! My parents would explain to me that I shouldn't let it bother me, and that I should find my own way in life and not worry about what anyone said about it.

This attitude about not worrying what people thought of me was one of the greatest gifts my parents ever gave me, and I know

AFFECTION

they couldn't realize just how far I would take the idea. This caused me to begin to listen impartially to other people's opinions, and try to figure out how they came to their decisions.

Well the years passed, and my grandfather never changed the way he treated me. He always told me that I was growing up as a girl. I grew up in the sixties, a time when long hair was in style and people were starting to question the old ways. He was beside himself as he saw that I had decided to grow my hair long and he'd say; "now all you need is a dress". His total disappointment in me was now complete.

I struggled for many years with how he treated me and picked me apart. After all these years, I have finally understood what my grandfather was trying to teach me. I know he was very cruel and to some people this may sound like I'm making an excuse for him, but believe me I don't condone his ways at all. It took me a long time to see the reasoning behind all of the personal attacks.

My grandfather had gone about it all wrong, but it was his way and the only way he knew how to teach me. We are never sure how someone is going to take our advice, and I guess I could give him a break, since he probably didn't know who Sigmund Freud was. What did my grandfather know about psychology? He tried his best to do what he believed was the right thing to do.

I look back now on how hard it was to have a grandfather that was so tough on me, until I learned to see really why he did what he did. I took up and excelled in the Japanese martial art of judo, and after much hard work, was ranked in the top eight in the United States. My grandfather took this to mean that I could stand up for what I believed in.

FIND YOUR WAY

This understanding came from the time reference of his own upbringing, that a man had to know how to fight for what he had, and believed in. To me this seemed like such an out dated requirement to meet, but to him it was all-important. Once my grandfather learned of my accomplishment, his attitude changed towards me.

After he believed I'd become the man he always wanted me to be, he was a totally different person toward me. He told me about people, places and things in his long life, and how it affected him and his hope for me, and the future of our family. Only then did I realize how important family was to my grandfather. He didn't just see his family and his kids; he saw our entire family as his legacy. My grandfather continued to shape and mold the family in his own way, until the day he died. Working to make us into the people he believed we should be.

My grandfather died at the age of one hundred, and I miss his insight into a different time and a totally different view of life. Looking back, I would have bet nearly anything growing up, that it wouldn't have been my grandfather that I hear in my daily life, but I was wrong. I often still hear him in my mind, teaching me those life lessons he so wanted our family to learn. He was not an eloquent man, but he did have some important wisdom to impart.

Along with this insight into my own life, we find an important life lesson that everyone has something to share, some wisdom, if we are able to hear it over our own personal dysfunctions. In fact, if we just pay a bit of attention, we will realize that everyone that touches our life can teach us something. We have an ingrained habit of taking everything as a personal attack upon us, and if we are able to overcome this bout of ego esteem, we are then capable of catching the meaning of our everyday lessons.

AFFECTION

One more important thing that I have learned in life, is to take what is good from the people that you meet, and discard the unpleasant. This is like eating a bad meal and forgetting about the great dessert, at least something good came of it.

8

Assumptions

Fear, caused by our imagination creates all kinds of problems for us, such as when we are in a social situation, we may feel anxious or threatened. This is the paradox of ego esteem that we don't believe in ourselves, so we feel threatened by our environment, but it is only our imagination that has created our fear.

We are the only ones that can control our fear, so we must not belittle ourselves in our own mind, because it is this very mind of ours that is telling us that we are not good enough. We are the creators of our own self-esteem, which is essentially the belief in ourselves. Again the paradox, we are the creator and the destroyer of our own personal self-esteem all wrapped up in one. We eagerly listen to our self-doubt as it plays back to us in our mind, causing us to doubt ourselves. So the question is, why should we listen to the voice that wants us to fail or feel inferior?

Other people may have caused us to believe that we don't measure up to a certain standard, but it's up to us to make ourselves believe it or not. When we begin to doubt ourselves and fall into the trap of negative thinking, we must stop and

ASSUMPTIONS

analyze the reason why we feel inferior or belittled. The problem often does not lie with us personally, but can be found in the struggle of other people's ego-esteem issues. Someone in our life may have had to have center stage, and to make him or herself feel more important, they proceeded to belittle us, to take back the spotlight.

When our mind runs it's internal dialog, and we start to question ourselves and everyone around us, our imagination takes over and we begin to create our own false reality, with ourselves as the victim. When we begin to live from our imagination, negative thoughts of suspicion and anger begin to control our perceptions. When we begin to work off these negative assumptions, we start to build our lives on what we assume. If all the assumptions are correct, then we have made the right decisions, however we could be completely wrong because assumptions are really just guesses.

One of our biggest mistaken assumptions is that everyone thinks like me. So most of the decisions that we make are based on the way we think. This of course leads us to assume that what's good for us is good for everyone else. So when we jump to a particular conclusion about something, it is based on what we want it to be and this is the definition of an egocentric person.

Let's say that your boss comes in mad, do you think it might be your fault? Or if your spouse is mad, is your first thought that it might be your fault? You can imagine anything, and I mean anything. If we let this kind of thinking control our minds, we are lost in a fantasy world of our own design, and in this false reality the only truth is our suspicions of people and our imagination. At this point our suspicion and imagination has taken control of our life, and we end up with only assumptions and no solid facts. We begin to be suspicious of everything and everybody, which feeds our illusion.

We can only speculate on what other people are thinking, because there is no way of truly knowing what somebody else is thinking, unless they actually tell us. Living by speculation is really a hard way to live. If we speculate about other people's motives, we are probably judging them against our own motives. Most people mirror others through their motives, thinking that everyone does things for the same reason we do. This is only telling what we would or should have done, not what really happened. This is unfair to everyone that we judge against what we imagine is true.

People often take perception and align it with personality, which makes up our gut feelings. This is part of our internal dialog that can convince us that we are unimportant, fat, ugly, or anything that we can imagine. This internal voice runs on and on, and plays over again and again, repeating all the insecurities we have. Once we understand that we are continuously repeating what we have been told from an abusive personality, we can recognize that it is only ourselves repeating it over and over again in our head, trying to convince ourselves that it's true.

This repeating voice creates pain within us as we continuously relive the abuse over and over again. If we don't recognize this voice as our own, and begin to change our thinking, then we will carry this pain with us forever. It's the pattern of pain that keeps us repeating it, and if we hear it enough, we will believe it. It doesn't matter if someone else is saying it, or if we are repeating it over and over again in our own mind, we are still hearing it. This is where we learn not to believe in ourselves.

ASSUMPTIONS

We may have been influenced from a young age to think of ourselves in a certain way by our family and friends, but its up to us to convince ourselves if it is true. This is where positive denial comes in, and it can be an up hill battle, but it is the way to change our thinking. Once we analyze our behavior and the other people around us, we begin to understand that abuse often comes from someone else struggling to find their importance. When we see that the abuser is most often the alpha personality in the family or social group, and that they tear down others to establish their importance, then we can realize that the fault does not always lie with us.

The alpha personality needs to feel superior to others because as we saw in a previous chapter, they must boost their ego esteem and they use everyone that is available to do this. We have to realize that most of the things that they say is part of an agenda that isn't true. It is hard to deal with people who have insecurities because in all kinds of different ways, we feel that we must yield to keep from injuring them. The alpha personality wants us to be less confident and give up our self-interest to them. Alpha's are often threatened by someone who is self-confident because they realize that they have no control over that person.

People with insecurities look at a person with self-confidence as a threat, because they are always comparing themselves to others. They see the self-confidence person as secure about themselves, and in comparison it makes them feel inferior. If we are insecure, anxious or nervous, then our imagination has convinced us that something is substandard. So someone with self-confidence is a threat, because they are not showing this substandard feeling.

The way to fix this problem is to simply quit repeating the abusive dialog to yourself. It sounds to good to be true, but the

FIND YOUR WAY

long and short of it is, that if you can repeat a negative thought over and over again, then why cant you repeat something positive over and over? Imagination is a wonderful thing, most people will tell us that imagination has never failed them, because we can imagine anything we want, be it real or not. Our internal dialog can be what other people have said to us, or what we imagine it is, its up to us to make our own reality.

Imagination helps us to see how we would choose an outcome, or how we think things could happen, so we tend to filter everything through our desire for a certain outcome. The question of imagination is based on our desire to have things go our way. Desire is only hoping for things to turn out great for us, because it's nearly impossible to have everyone's desires fulfilled at the same time. This is because if we could fulfill everyone's desire, then we would be everything to everyone.

If we imagine the worst thing possible and fixate on it, then you make this thing come to reality. If you are worried about your husband cheating on you and you look at everything he does and question him about your suspicions, this makes him feel that he might as well do it, because he has already been accused as a cheat. This could actually make what you fear most come to reality, because your own imagination has created a self-fulfilling prophecy.

So, while trying to get your reassurances, you drive him further away because if you don't trust him, then you are questioning his love for you, and his self respect. The questions come from your own insecurity, and not his behavior. If you question him all the time, then you are telling him that he is not trustworthy.

Think back and try to remember where the internal dialog started, someone said something that may or may not have

ASSUMPTIONS

been true. We must question the reason why we heard the abuse, and where it came from. It may have come from someone else's ego esteem issues or immaturity problems.

Remember, that dysfunction comes in many forms, and that abuse, disrespect and immaturity are the most common. It has always amazed me personally to see grown adults demean someone because they are obese, I have actually seen adults laugh and point at obese people and make fun of them.

I was once going through the White House tour in Washington D.C., and heard someone remark about a blind person on the tour. The man said, "Why is he going"? The blind man quickly retorted, "they do *describe* the things on the tour". It was not very mature for someone to demean the blind man, but it happens everyday. This is a matter of maturity. This reminds us to pay close attention to the people we are trusting for their opinions; it may not be worth listening to them.

So just consider the source of the abuse that caused the insecurity. If what we have been told about ourselves isn't true, then ignore it. Remember that the alpha personality, ego-esteem person, and the abusive personality find their value when they make others feel devalued. Understanding that abusive remarks tend to come from people who have dysfunctional personalities themselves, then listening to their opinion is ridiculous. Repeating the derogatory remarks over and over in our mind from people who have more problems than we do is not a recipe for a happy and functional life.

9

Manipulation

All kinds of people have fallen under the spell of a dysfunctional person even the ones that are considered very competent, even tempered with good coping skills, and a sense of humor have been convinced that they are the dysfunctional one.

When we live through our insecurities and fears we see life differently from people with good self-esteem. Those of us that struggle with insecurities feel as if everyone is out to get us. Through our insecurities we perceive threats that don't exist, because paranoia is the next natural step as we attempt to predict problems before they happen. This behavior makes us look for the same type of situation to happen again.

Our insecurities push us into protection mode around everyone, and our overcompensating projects our insecurity onto everyone around us, showing that we are uncomfortable. When we feel uncomfortable in social situations, it makes us grasp at our friends or spouse for protection. Insecurities are like having a sore thumb that we are always very worried about hitting again.

When we worry about hitting our thumb, that worry nearly guarantees that we will hit it. It's like looking for, or predicting

MANIPULATION

that something bad is going to happen to us before it does. Once we program the insecurity into our mind through our internal dialog, we virtually guarantee that it will happen. It's the same thing as when someone says, "Whatever you do, don't think of pink elephants." This guarantees that we will think of pink elephants.

When we overcompensate for our insecurities, we tend to look for someone or something to help defend us. What we are asking is for someone to defend our imagined worry about something that doesn't exist. From whatever quarter our insecurity has come from in the past, we will be on guard from it happening to us again, and when these insecurities are triggered, this is where we look for others to do whatever it takes to make us feel safe. This is the beginning of changing everyone around us for our own self-interest. So, it would be the most natural thing to do then, to make the people we love into what we think is loving and caring even if it's dysfunctional.

Through our insecurities, we feel that our partner should brace us up against our feelings of insecurity. What we need may be more attention, and we expect our partner to give us all the attention that we need to feel secure. If this need for feeling safe and secure isn't fulfilled, then we feel that we are not being taken care of, and that our partner is not being attentive to our needs.

This is where a person's insecurity becomes the proof of our love, and if we don't help to continue the dysfunction, then we don't love them. When a dysfunctional person wants attention, they have no problem manipulating our emotions to fill their desire for attention.

FIND YOUR WAY

One way to fill the desire for emotional attention is by making us responsible for someone else's emotional well being through feelings of guilt. They will use the guilt to get the attention they desire, and this makes them feel important. They make us feel guilty by explaining that the way we feel is wrong, and that we should be there for them whenever they need us.

This leaves the person that is being manipulated by guilt feeling displeased. The feeling of guilt causes the person to try to overcompensate for not being perceived as caring. The insecure person explains how we the guilty person or enabler, should feel. The dysfunctional person makes us feel guilty for not feeling the same way as they do, insuring the reaction they want, which is manipulating our feelings so that they can insure their control over our belief of helping.

What makes our feelings wrong, compared to someone who has all their feelings come from insecurities? Remember the definition of a dysfunctional person. This leads us right into what the guilt was used for, mainly all the attention that the insecure person believes they deserve. We feel shame, because we feel guilty.

When we have two conflicting emotions at the same time, we are ambiguous about our feelings, and once this emotional manipulation is continued over and over again to get the desired results, we become emotionally confused about our true emotional reactions. If guilt is used against us over and over again, we become hypersensitive, causing us to be constantly on guard from not wanting to feel guilt and shame.

By becoming hypersensitive, we always end up apologizing for not living up to the dysfunctional persons expectations. We have to feed the desire of the person that needs the attention, or

MANIPULATION

have guilt laid on us. Who wants to feel the shame that someone makes us feel because we forgot to do something, or how many times have we had to say, "I am sorry" to someone who demands so much of us? If the words I am sorry come constantly from us because someone is unhappy, then we may have become a crutch for that someone's emotional well being.

This may lead us to feel as if we were an uncaring person, which will eventually cause us to demean ourselves. We must remember, that the dysfunctional person's agenda is to have us feel the same way as they do, which leads us to be dysfunctional as well. Insecurity is a fear based emotional state that comes from an imagined perceived idea, and this is the idea that they are asking us to share with them, causing us to fall into the same hole as them.

Another manipulation tactic is pity, like when someone tells us something that makes us feel sorry for him or her. Here again, we are manipulated into feeling a certain way, which causes us to give our attention to someone. When the insecure person has to manipulate others to fulfill themselves, then they are damaging the other people in their life.

Once again, the paradox is that the more we use emotional blackmail, the less affective it becomes. How many times can someone be blackmailed until it doesn't work anymore? How many times are you going to be told how you should feel?

This is the people pleasers nightmare, where the emotional roller coaster begins. We feel shame for feeling guilty and we feel demeaned because we are not pleasing someone. The dysfunctional person knows we don't want to feel that we are not pleasing them, and are convinced that they know how we should react.

FIND YOUR WAY

If we don't live by the rules of dysfunction then we don't care. We become attached to this person's dysfunctional emotional eruptions and once again; become the crutch for the emotional well being of another person.

We have all been on the receiving end of guilt, but the trick is to understand the desired agenda and not to give in. This may lead people to believe that we are heartless, but if we listen carefully, we will hear only the sounds of self-pity.

I remember a friend of mine, that every time his girlfriend would get mad at him, he would have to do something extreme to make her happy again. When I asked him why he would go to such lengths for her, he would always reply that I just wouldn't understand. In this dysfunctional relationship, he had to give her extraordinary amounts of attention to make her feel safe. If he didn't do this, then she made him feel that he just didn't care for her, and his outlandish behavior was her proof that he did love her.

We all know a couple that if one of them is busy talking in a group of friends or family, the other will go and interrupt the conversation and complain that they are not paying enough attention to them. This happens even if the partner hasn't seen their family or friends for a long time, and is just catching up on what's going on in each other's lives, or when family members reminiscence about each other growing up. If a co-dependent is left alone and isn't included in the conversation, then they feel unimportant. The dysfunctional person needs another person to prove that they care for them and interrupting insures the reaction from their partner.

So the partner goes into the care-taking mode to fulfill the requirements of the relationship. This is a dysfunctional person

MANIPULATION

making a competent person into a dysfunctional person. The competent person is told over and over again that they are uncaring if they don't meet the needs of the dysfunctional person. If we don't understand that being insecure and feeling unimportant is a result of our own dysfunctional belief, then we think it's because someone outside ourselves is responsible. This behavior is only enabling the dysfunction to continue.

When someone uses our emotional attachment to him or her to make us do something for them, its called blackmail. How many times have we heard someone use this type of blackmail to persuade a reluctant partner to have sex? "If you really cared about me, then you wouldn't hesitate to share our love".

They know emotionally that we don't want to deny them anything, even if it's not such a good idea. It is pitting emotions against logic, but still it doesn't matter because it is the co-dependents job to continually guard the amount of attention that is required to feel significant. Our idea of importance is to demand an inordinate amount of attention to make us feel valued. Co-dependents tend to cling to each other in a social setting because of their dependence on each other for the reassurance of importance.

In co-dependent families, many dysfunctional behaviors are excused because without each other, each member is on their own. This makes everyone else outside the co-dependent circle upset, because of the amount of attention that is required to make him or her feel important. Most everyone is confused when the dysfunctional person gets mad and complains that they are being unappreciated. When our self-esteem is so bad that we have to shut out the entire world and have our partner reinforce us, then it is clearly a co-dependent, dysfunctional relationship.

FIND YOUR WAY

Then to believe that we are the functional person in this relationship and to make our friends, family, or partner change to fit our idea of a caring relationship is wrong. But if it's all we know, it seems like the right thing to do.

If our family is dysfunctional then this becomes a battle between who is more important, our new relationship, or our family. The dysfunctional view is that our family is always going to be there for us, and even though this is true, it causes undue friction between them and our new family.

When all the family's attention is focused on the head of the family, then we are entering into someone's little kingdom, and into a relationship with a dysfunctional family. In this relationship we will find that everything we do will have to be cleared by the head of the family. If a co-dependent wants approval they will ask their family to intervene on their behalf, causing friction between the co-dependent family and the new family. This effectively removes the important natural boundaries between the families and prevents the couple from learning to work out their own problems.

Everything becomes the dysfunctional families business, because the dysfunctional family is the co-dependent's base of approval. If a co-dependent needs reinforcement of their behavior, then they will naturally go first to the family who taught them that behavior. This is one of the main reasons that dysfunctional families cling together so closely, because of the understanding and reinforcement that they get from each other. When we reassure each other's behavior, it couldn't possibly be wrong because everyone in the dysfunctional family agrees.

If it is set up as a little kingdom, then everyone must bow to the king. It is understandable that a member of a dysfunctional

MANIPULATION

family wants the same setup as their family. When you must have another person reinforce your deficiencies, then you are asking them to be dysfunctional too. When emotional demands are incomprehensible, where is the logic of giving in to these demands?

This is asking someone to give in to our emotional and impractical demands to assume emotional responsibility. This builds up the dependency that they will need us which gives us power, insuring that our partner won't leave us. This is emotional manipulation and it makes our partner subordinate to us so that they must have us around.

This is the feeling of importance of the caretaker. When we manipulate someone to get the response we want then this is not real emotion, it's a control or blackmail emotion. Everything about this emotion has been fabricated, so we will have manipulated the outcome. With this, we have successfully distorted reality into some self-serving dysfunction, and changed most of our friends and lovers into this dysfunction.

This is our standard of love, being the caretaker of our anxiety, fears, and imagination. This is a job and not a love affair.

10

Self-Esteem

When we have real self esteem that is based on what is true about ourselves, then it matters very little what people say about us. If we are called a thief and it's not true, then we can live with it, because we know the truth. False accusations really shouldn't bother us, because our self-esteem isn't based on approval, or what people think of us. It really doesn't matter what people think, because they are going to believe what they want to believe. This is the true battle for our self-esteem.

If we have poor self-esteem and we meet a person with good self-esteem, what would it make us feel like? Maybe we would feel inferior, deficient, inadequate or weak, because poor self-esteem is based on comparison.

Many people with poor self-esteem have been belittled most of their lives, so to them belittling others is normal. To protect ourselves from what we feel as a threat to our comparison of esteem, finding fault with the other person would become very important. If we can find fault, then it will degrade the other person, and we wont have to compare our self with them. This starts the evaluation of people from the moral high ground on which we believe we stand, giving us the right to discount outright the opinion of the other person.

SELF-ESTEEM

It's our natural reaction to defend ourselves from pain and anxiety, so if we can find something wrong, then the other person's opinion won't be considered valuable.

It is this belief in comparison that we must consider in our own opinion about other people. If we have an agenda to find something that we don't like about another person, then just to protect our own esteem, we will definitely find something. It is from the protection of their poor self esteem that we will hear the dysfunctional person say anything to make us feel inadequate ourselves.

Once the people with poor self-esteem have set themselves up to be an authority on morality, then everyone must pass their test of correct behavior. We have probably all heard someone comment that we did something they wouldn't do, and by doing this, they see us as less than they are. It is a disparaging comment designed to make another feel less than they are. Just remember, when someone is calling us names, or trying to put us down, it is a response from a defense mechanism.

Let's say someone has called us fat and ugly. We have a pretty good idea that the person who called us fat and ugly has low self-esteem, because it's not a respectable thing to say. What we need to understand is that the person who is making this comment is not respectful of other people, and is being abusive by showing their character flaws. It is hard to listen to such people, but once we understand that this person has a dysfunction, then we must learn to forgive them for their behavior.

If it's not respectful or honorable or kind, then it is the opposite of good self-esteem, which makes this person dysfunctional, and people who laugh with them, show that they have a problem as well. Really, this type of behavior can be summed up as a maturity problem, and we will find that even adults often have problems with maturity.

It is the people with little or no coping skills that are the ones that we should sympathize with, because their whole life is filled with discontent. If someone has trouble coping with life, then trying to manage a relationship and to realize his or her hopes and dreams is greatly limited.

Now lets look at the difference between being assertive and aggressive. Being assertive is standing up for what we believe, and being aggressive is to attack or defend someone or something, usually in a demeaning way. Being assertive we know that we have the right to be treated with respect and dignity, and we demand to not be put down, demeaned or devalued. Being aggressive we are protecting our self-esteem, and insulting to get our point across.

The attitude of aggression comes with attacks on others designed to defend a fragile ego. This attitude of aggression has its defense mechanism at play, namely, that we are out to defend and protect ourselves because we have been belittled, humiliated, embarrassed, or devalued in the past, so we respond with the belief that we are being attacked again.

What makes criticism and advice different? Why is it when we don't like what people say it's called criticism, and if we do like it it's called advice. What is the difference? Both are opinions and both are critiquing us; the question is how do we take it? Does it hurt or not, or in other words does it hurt our feelings or our ego?

SELF-ESTEEM

It makes all the difference in the world on whom the critique is coming from and whether we like that person or not. The way we feel about that person will greatly effect our perception of the critique, so what is this telling us? If we consider the opinion and it's true it's true. If we consider it and it's not true, then why should it bother us? How we perceive the critique and our reactions to it is a direct reflection of our ego-esteem. If we surround ourselves with people that reinforce what we want to hear, then we are not looking for the truth, we are just looking to find someone to enable our behavior or beliefs.

Being able to choose our reactions and not fly off the handle is a sure sign of good coping skills. The inability to control our self in a heated argument is a sign of ego-esteem. The truest and fastest way to test someone's coping skills is an all out attack on a person, be it verbal or physical. When everything spirals out of control and leads us into situations that we really don't want to happen, then we have a problem with coping skills.

A co-dependent suppresses their anger and sooner or later it comes out in a passive aggressive manner. While suppressing their anger it starts to boil inside them and it might be days or weeks or even months until they lash out.

This is the reason for an impulsive response, which is another self defense mechanism. With the feeling of having to defend ourselves, we lash out to get our point across. We might feel that we have been wronged in some way and that we must be on the defensive. The more we feel that we have to defend, the more passive aggressive we become. Defending what we believe is valuable becomes a life long anticipation against perceived attacks. This can become a reason for being overly sensitive to other's remarks, setting up hostile motives and defensive responses.

FIND YOUR WAY

Since most co-dependents repress their anger, this passive aggressive anger may be perceived as normal and is ignored, ensuring that the hostile motive never gets questioned. When disrespectful attitudes are the norm in our lives, we don't question them when being either disrespectful or disrespected. Do we have control when we can't show our anger because we will be perceived as weak and out of control? Who deals with anger better, the person who gets mad and finishes it, or the one who holds it in for weeks and then does something to get even?

The people pleaser is afraid to show anger, because it is the facade that they judge their own life with the goal of being popular, and to question this belief system is questioning their own value. So most of the time this person will throw these snide little remarks at people. These disparaging remarks come from old anger that has been held on to and then leaks out. It's the desire to get even and no one likes these snide passive aggressive remarks. If we deal with anger when it arises, then there will be no need for it to sneak out in other ways.

If we don't deal with our anger in a healthy strait forward way, then we are riding the emotional roller coaster and have no control over our responses to any given situation. When we don't have control over our emotions then we are explosive. Saying or doing the wrong thing around this person will set them off on a tangent of explosive behavior, causing everyone that knows them to walk around on eggshells, so as not to make them mad. This type of control at the point of a gun is not a good way to live.

When we think we have control over others this makes us feel powerful, and once we start this, it is very hard to stop. The perception of what we believe is control is actually abuse. Control from a threat of reprisal, with verbal or physical abuse is

SELF-ESTEEM

backward and cowardly, because without this perception of control we are afraid of not being in charge and getting our way. When someone uses intimidation to control people they are just being a bully, and what should we do with a bully? We have to stand up for ourselves and confront them, because we all know that bullies are really just cowards hiding behind a façade of bravado.

When we deny that things are bothering us and we get temperamental, everyone around us has to suffer for our lack of coping skills. This is the person that when asked what's wrong they answer nothing, but find that everything we do is annoying them, and this irritation often leads to a confrontation. This is someone who is trying to deny their feelings, and it makes them irritable because they won't deal with their problems, which makes it very hard to live with them. We must realize, that the only way to have a dysfunctional relationship is with other dysfunctional people.

Moods are designed to have a particular affect, and how many times have we heard someone say, " be careful, he is not in a good mood". This is a desired affect, gained by manipulating others by our mood into the way we want them to treat us because we are feeling unhappy. This allows us to comfortably feel sorry for ourselves, and becomes our very own pity party, where everyone we come into contact with is expected to attend.

Then comes the embarrassment of finding out that we are dysfunctional. When we realize the truth, we immediately try to hide it from everyone, and when it is discovered, we tend to lash out from behind our insecurity to defend our dysfunction. It is very hard to come to grips with a dysfunction, because it wants to be left alone to flourish. Denial is the emotional barrier to realizing the truth, which directly reflects our ego.

FIND YOUR WAY

We don't want it to be true, so we deny its existence. This is the ego-esteem struggling to survive, and it really feels like someone is trying to hurt us.

In some traditions, those who have experienced killing the ego-esteem refer to it as the great death. By accomplishing this seemingly insurmountable feat, we are counted among the truly strong and find that by no longer allowing our dysfunctions to mislead us, we are finally able to tackle the big things in life.

11

Justification

People who must have their feelings validated are trying to protect themselves from not feeling important. However, they do feel important enough to verify their belief through their feelings. Because their feelings are important to them, they think it should be important to others. This is the idea of ego-esteem values.

If we have an ethical or moral point, then our feelings are validated. We believe that through justifying our feelings, we give others a reason to pay attention to us by earning our keep. Are we asking someone to agree with the importance of our feelings, or are we asking them to consider our feelings? It's not the question of emotion, but of the motive. If we have an agenda behind the emotion, then the emotion is a tool that we will try to use to convince other people. This is the real reason we want consideration of an emotion.

If we can get people to agree with the importance of our feelings, then we perceive that it is enough to prove our position. This is finding value in our feelings and not through our beliefs. We have the right to feel any way that we want to, but it doesn't mean that it will give us any validity.

JUSTIFICATION

The idea of making a point to someone where it becomes the most important thing is an emotional connection, which only identifies the subject but not the substance of the problem. It is placing the importance on our emotions, rather than finding a resolution to the problem. If our point is an emotional attachment to that particular problem and not the resolution, then our importance was the emotion.

Here is an example; some people say that we can't disagree with our government's policies and still be a good citizen, the old love it or leave it policy. It is the emotional importance of allegiance to country rather than the substance of the freedom to disagree. When we are out flag waving and denouncing a freedom, then we are saying that it's wrong to disagree with the emotion that is tied to the allegiance of the country. There is so much emotional ferocity connected with a country's image, that this is the reason that some countries are trying to get nuclear weapons. To pursue these weapons is looked upon as national pride or an emotional value. We see this as a threat to everyone else in the world, but it makes the country feel proud to have some esteem in the world by having these weapons.

This is one of the reasons that most of us can't understand the religious brutality of other countries. The zealots are seeking the feeling that comes from the honor of taking their own lives as they kill others for the glory of God. When the emotional attachment begins to overwhelm the reality of the real message, then the emotion will magnify the situation. How much does religious excitement affect you? By the emotional attachment to your particular religion and the furious protection of your faith, how far would you go to protect it? This is the problem with people feeling the importance to the emotional investment in a subject. Once emotion is all that counts, it doesn't require reason to prove an emotional point.

FIND YOUR WAY

This is one of the many reasons it's hard to account for the viability of emotions in an argument. We must recognize the emotional investment of the person, but it can't outweigh the real reasoning. The emotional investment in a cause, religion or country should be recognized for what it is, an emotional investment. If it's important to me, then it must be important.

How many countries have used an emotional investment to prove their right to do monstrous events? One comes to mind real quick, Germany during world wars one and two. There really is a long list of countries that have whipped their citizens into an emotional frenzy, but unfortunately none of it had to do with reality, and it still happens. When we base an argument on our feelings about that subject, than the reality of the subject no longer matters. It is the understanding that emotion rides on feelings, and logic rides on reasoning.

Few people want to discipline their child because of their emotional attachment, but it's beneficial for them. Once we understand that it's for the child's own good, then the emotional attachment must take a back seat to the benefits. When kindness enables people to do what they want because they know that we identify with being kind, then it becomes our way of feeling valuable. Only when we begin to confuse kindness for enabling, does the trouble begin.

The enabler thinks that they are doing this to be good and kind, but they are actually insuring their own happiness by being the good guy. When kindness becomes the problem, then it's no longer kind. Like not disciplining your children, because it makes you feel bad. This feeling bad allows the children to grow up without any social boundaries that would make them better human beings. This is the time when emotional investment must be put into its proper place.

JUSTIFICATION

Kindness comes from wanting to feel good about ourselves and to be seen as a good caring person. This then becomes just another way to find validation in our lives. Kindness is best when we know that it will effect the change that is needed, like the call for random acts of kindness just for kindness sake. This type of kindness looks for no recognition and truly is for someone else, and not for the effect it gives to the giver.

When our kindness is used as a weapon to ensure others dysfunction, then people that know us will use this feeling against us to get what they want. This is the child that knows mom just can't say no, so all they have to do is complain enough to get what they want. This kindness is now a weapon, an emotional tug of war with logic and approval that becomes one of the emotional mind games that we play with ourselves, by validating our feelings for the sake of validation.

12

Love

When it comes to love and attraction, are we at the mercy of our subconscious when we choose our partner? There are many theories about what attracts us to our mates, for instance there is a theory that some of us look at the shape of a person, or that a certain physical characteristic draws us because of a subconscious signal attracting us to the other's particular gene pool. We could literally be drawn to somebody because subconsciously we are attracted to his or her genes.

Since all the chemicals and hormones that are released at puberty is a new experience for the teenage brain, falling in love as a teenager is a much more dramatic encounter than in adulthood. This first love experience can be quite overwhelming which makes for a much more intense attraction phase then is typically undergone by adults. Girls are less likely to get involved in sexual activity unless their social environment encourages it, but for boys the high levels of testosterone can often lead to early sexual activity.

There are certain chemicals and hormones released in the brain when we fall in love. When this happens, it is comparable to having a mental illness. When it comes to love, one of the great driving forces is biochemistry.

LOVE

Lust is driven by the sex hormones testosterone and estrogen, and the testosterone that is produced by the male, plays a major role in the sex drive. There are studies that have shown that falling in love has a similar effect on the brain as cocaine, because the effects are so pleasurable it can become an addiction.

When people fall in love they can think of nothing else, loosing their appetite and the need for sleep, becoming completely enthralled with their new lover. But once they have been together for a while, they begin to form attachments to each other and the relationship becomes more stable, creating a long lasting bond that keeps couples together. There are two hormones that contribute significantly to long-term relationships; they are called oxytocin and vasopressin, which are released by the nervous system

Here is the catch, if we have been devalued and not shown respect by our parents, then how would we evaluate love? With low self-esteem, we would seek attention to feed the desire to feel valuable. The problem is if we don't feel valuable with a good sense of self-esteem, then attention gets confused with love. This desire for attention directs us to think that the attention is enough. Love of attention is basing our desire on the need to be valued, and not on the fact that we are valuable.

 To fall in love with someone because we admire and respect them as a person is basing love on valuable characteristics. We can admire our partner because of the choices they make by being honest, truthful, compassionate, and respectful. These are the things that make us all feel valuable.

Some of us consider a love partner to be the one that completes us by fulfilling our inadequacies, making the idea of love an embodiment of emotional and physical welfare. What we are saying is that we are getting into a relationship as only half a person, and giving someone else the responsibility to make us whole.

Many people only feel that they are in love when they are needed, that they are essential to the other person, a crutch. The significance of being the important one in the relationship is love to some people. To question these things is important, so that we understand if we are looking for strength or weakness in a relationship. If we are looking for strength, then we know that the person chooses us because they want to, instead of choosing us out of need, in the case of weakness. Need is not a good reason to get involved with someone.

When it's attention that we crave, it turns into a physical characteristic. When love is based on attention, the focus becomes distorted because we desire the attention, and not the respect of our character. This is looking for someone to give us value, and the feeling that someone is showing us a lot of attention. The attention that is given us boosts our esteem and feels so good.

When it's the public display of attention that makes us feel that we are in love, then it is merely having our needs met on a superficial level. It is this confusion of feeling good about having our esteem boosted, rather than being respected and admired. If our partner treats us with respect and admiration, then they shouldn't have to prove their love. This is the difference between seeking attention and knowing the real reason that we are loved. Once again, if we have to have someone else to make us feel good about ourselves, then it becomes dysfunctional. When we confuse attention with love, then we are leaving out the most important things in a relationship.

LOVE

The attention that we receive stimulates a physical response making it a superficial reaction. When we desire a physical stimulant, be it drugs, food or sex, we are trying to fulfill our need for value. The physical excitement of the particular stimulant activates many different parts of the body. The adrenal gland causes the dopamine in the brain to flow, which gives us euphoric feelings similar to a person who uses drugs, alcohol, food, or sex. This physical response may easily be mistaken as a real feeling of love.

When our love is based on attention, then the easiest way to get physical attention in a relationship is by having sex. The problem is how many times can we be intimate with different people before we lose the capacity to be intimate? How many special people would we have in our life? The loss of intimacy makes it very hard on that one special person that we have chosen to make a life with.

When people over eat or drink too much, they often say it's because they want to feel comforted. Food never denies the feeling of fulfillment to the over eater, and alcohol never denies the feeling of forgetting your problems. It is the reason that many people fail at long-term relationships, because when the excitement of the new love affair is over, they feel empty.

How long can the drugs of the mind continue to affect us once the physical attention stops? This is why the physical stimulant has been distorted by what we feel as love. When we create these certain conditioned responses, we want to act on them because without the responses we are lost. How many of us have been in love and has seen what we want to see? When we are in love, the chemicals in the brain are stimulated and affected to the point of excitement, exhilaration and anticipation. Are we thinking clearly?

FIND YOUR WAY

The Serotonin that our brain releases may actually make us temporarily insane, so are we going to see what we want to see and pay little or no attention to what is really going on? People get attached to these feelings and when they are gone, they think that they have fallen out of love. These chemicals produce wonderful feelings, but they only last so long. When the effects have worn off, there needs to be something that we respect about our partner, something concrete.

It is the release of endorphins that creates the idea that man and women weren't meant to stay together for a lifetime. It is the excitement of a new relationship that releases the endorphins that makes us feel so good. It is the anticipation of the release of endorphins that make men and women look for that new love in their life. It leads people to think that the feelings that they had for one another has disappeared, when it is only us getting use to the release of endorphins. This should cause people to rethink the original attraction that led them into their relationships. If it is the attraction to the endorphins released by the excitement of a new love interest, then we are looking for a new relationship for the wrong reasons. Is the addiction to the rush of endorphins more important to us than a true in depth, fulfilling relationship?

Ending a relationship starts all the defense mechanism that can occur from a heart felt breakup, bringing to bear all the old emotional baggage that a person has gathered from prior relationships. The resentments of past lovers are the consequences that many people have to deal with on a daily basis.

The paradox of love and sex is that we want to be as close as we can with the person that we love, but if the relationship fails, then it gets harder and harder to open ourselves up for the next

LOVE

love in our life. Remember that Intimacy involves openness, sharing and trust that contribute to maturity. We live in the place of paradox. How can anyone get to know us if we are always guarding ourselves? No one can know us because we're to busy guarding ourselves from the outside world. If we are afraid to fall totally in love because we think that someone might hurt us, then we can't give of ourselves totally. If we fear being put down or being embarrassed, then we are not going to say anything that might put ourselves in jeopardy.

If we keep everyone at arms length, and fear that we won't get approval if we say what we really feel, then no one will ever know the real you. Not until we turn our fear about having our guard up into strength, will we become the person that we want to be, and break the cycle of contradictions in our life. If we say what we believe and people disapprove, then we are being true to what we believe.

We defend ourselves from fear, and in doing so we build a wall against our fears, the fear of abandonment, embarrassment, rejection, really the fear of anything. We try to protect ourselves from these fears real or imagined, so we throw up walls and that makes us feel protected. These walls project an attitude that first must be dealt with, before we can even begin to know another person.

This attitude protects us by keeping people from getting to know the real person. This keeps others from seeing the vulnerable side of us. This is not protection from these fears, it's only hiding from the fear, and in reality it drives many people away from us, increasing the chance of abandonment, embarrassment, or rejection with this attitude. The maddening cycle of fear drives us to hide, rather than to face our fear. How can we be intimate with anyone while guarding our fears? When there is no openness, sharing and trust, there can be no intimacy.

13

Attitude

Attitudes can become obstacles that we may carry with us our entire lives. We can have an attitude that someone has done us wrong, and carry it with us until the day we die. All that this attitude does is get in the way of our progressing to a better life. If we have resentment against a situation that happened to us many years ago, then anytime we are in a similar situation, our attitude naturally will be poor. We can't get around the attitude that it will be the same thing again. It becomes a self-defeating mood, because we can't forget, and it then becomes resentment.

When we find someone's attitude offensive, remember that they are acting out of resentment. When we see someone's attitude, we are seeing the effects of a painful memory. The person with the attitude problem should realize that it is a memory, something from the past and that they should not judge anything from the past. How far back in the past is the attitude coming from, a month, a year, or twenty? How would we like to be judged by what our great grandfather did? Is it a badge of honor to see how long we can hold a grudge?

There have been attacks on people because of grudges going back over a hundred years, stemming from something that may

ATTITUDE

or may not even be clearly remembered. No one that was hurt could have had anything to do with the original incident, but the grudge was what his or her grandparents had passed on.

For example, there were attacks on Turkish people for the Armenian genocide some eighty years after it had happened. Armenian people that had not even been born at the time of the genocide led the uprising, by using their emotional attachment to the past as their right for reprisal. When we live in the past our attitude is attached to something that we can only imagine, unless we were there. This is the power of resentment and attitude of the victim.

If we have a bad attitude from something in the past, then it is a barrier for the future and the now. We are attaching ourselves to something that is done, finished. How else can we retaliate but by having a bad attitude? With this bad attitude, we are now searching for a reason to instigate a confrontation. Because of the attitude that you have hurt me, now I'm going to get you back. Don't let something in the past destroy your future.

There must be a time for us to say, let's start fresh. But for people harboring resentments, it is very hard to forgive because this too can be seen as empowerment. Attitude authorizes us to play the victim. You victimized me, so I'm mad. How long can we play the victim? If we can't get over it, then we are looking to get something from being a victim. But with this, all we are doing is being held hostage from resentments and feeling victimized.

The emotional attachment to being the victim gives us an excuse to validate this attitude. If we try to drive our car by looking behind us in the rear view mirror, instead of looking forward to where we are going, the question becomes how many accidents will we have.

FIND YOUR WAY

It is like living in the past, and trying to predict the future from those past events. We must learn to live in the present moment, because what is happening right now is what counts.

When we decide to live in the victim mode, we live a life of what's behind us, rather than looking ahead. The view never changes from the victim's viewpoint. If you seek peace in your life, then let yourself forgive and forget, and understand that you are only hurting yourself with a negative attitude.

14

Freedom

Our subconscious emotions cause us to react to stimulus from the outside world, and because these emotions are buried in our subconscious mind, we are often taken by surprise by the way we react to some things. We must search for the root of these emotions, and once we find the reason for these subconscious emotions, we will find that they are only an excuse or validation to authorize the reason we feel the way that we do.

Finding the validation to authorize our feelings, is simply justifying the reason for the emotion. Once again, we work within the limits of our own interpretive beliefs of what's right and what's wrong. We are interjecting our beliefs on others, and it will be our own reasoning for being mad, happy, sad and so on.

We must detach ourselves and look at the problem with clarity. When we detach ourselves from the emotion and look at it as an individual entity, we will realize that it is only us that gives the emotion life. This is the difference between seeing the action rather than to live in the action, because when we live in an action we are ruled by that action. We all have a choice to react to any given situation, and to choose our reactions, so isn't it a good idea to react for a good reason?

FREEDOM

Let's say that we are driving down the highway and someone cuts us off. Naturally we get mad and this emotion quickly engulfs us. We are attached to the anger because we feel that we have the right to be mad, however all that this anger has done for us is to take away our stability and make us unhappy. Was the anger really worth the disruption in your life? Was the pay off worth it just to show that we are mad? Was the expression of anger worth it to us and anyone else in the car with us? No, just because we have the right to get mad, doesn't mean that it is worth the price of the anger. Once we separate our indignation from ourselves, we will see that it is a useless endeavor. Remember that we are the one that gives importance or acknowledgement to any situation, and understanding this we control the power that it has over us.

Anger can pass us by without affecting our emotional state of mind, because it is only an entity that doesn't contain our stability. Once we see that anger is it's own separate entity, we can deny its reality by seeing it as a circumstance that we accommodate, rather than something that fully encompasses us. Once we detach from anger we can deny it, and keep our stability of mind. This is bringing the subconscious to the conscious mind and dealing with it reasonably. We must do this with every circumstance in our life, and after awhile with continued practice, we will learn to disrupt the process and deny angers reality.

We must examine our emotions and see if they are based on what is really bothering us, or if we are dealing with disappointment. This disappointment comes from the anxiety that our desires or needs are not being met, because they may be so selfish that they shouldn't be met. We should always take a moment to see if we are thinking only of ourselves, because selfishness always leads to disappointment and pain.

FIND YOUR WAY

When we have to deal with each individual persons belief of what is expected or desired, then we lead a life of dealing with disappointment.

When we color life through our dysfunctions, pain and our human limitations, we make the world into our own delusion. We understand the world only by what we think is correct. With all the emotional baggage and pain, we distort the reality of life. Life is filtered through everything that affects us in our daily life, but once we can see the dysfunction and its effects, we understand that life is really what we make it.

If we can overcome the distractions and dysfunctions in our life, then we can become the observer. The observer is not affected by dysfunction, or with the ego-esteem. Once our attachment to outcomes is diminished and our expectations are recognized for what they represent, then we can start to see the world as it truly is. When our attachments are recognized for the selfish fulfillment of ourselves, and that expectations are only an extension of ego-esteem, then we can begin to see how much we live for an illusion.

The observer is without prejudice, agenda, attachments, emotionalism and ego-esteem, and then what really happens, has happened. This is the only way to experience the reality of the world, without the filters of the self getting in the way. The selflessness of existence is the purest truth, and the goal of life is to see truth, and understand its meanings and consequences.

To fully live life, and to rip apart the delusions of man and his ownership of consequences, is the goal of realism. We have seen the pain of ego-esteem and how this ownership leads to so many different consequences.

FREEDOM

So in knowing the consequences, it is in our power to either live in its intoxicating delusion, or strive to live in the observer's reality.

The ego-esteem has created the ultimate illusion, by convincing us that we are not fulfilled in life. We are already fulfilled, but the ego-esteem has made us confused between true fulfillment, and the feeling we get from the rush of endorphins. True fulfillment comes from the freedom from the fix of endorphins. That endorphin rush is what most people are looking for when boosting their ego-esteem, its what they crave. The release into true freedom comes to us once we are self aware enough to realize, that we are living for the fix of endorphins.

Once we see that it is our true feelings about our character that completes us and not our ego-esteem, then we can have true freedom. Freedom from the ego-esteem is not making our decisions or values based on social conditioning. Nothing is more then it is, and to see someone operating under this understanding is to realize that they are truly free. Fulfillment is the freedom from ego-esteem, because fulfillment is realizing that we are doing it for its pure purpose. When a person is fully self aware, he or she realizes why they are doing the things they are doing.

Many people who have had a near death experience, and have had time to reflect on their lives realize that most of their time had been taken up with pity, jealousies, and bickering. After that kind of enlightening experience, they change their way of life.

When we realize that we have the ability to decide what we accept as our reality, we can then clearly decide if we choose to listen to people that have their own dysfunctional ways or not.

FIND YOUR WAY

Living our life through the ups and downs of others, and trying to fulfill their needs by denying our true self, is the choice of either being the codependent, or having a life of discovery. It is the choice of living in delusion, or having understanding and wisdom. It is how we accept the reality of our own existence, or the belief of another's view of how we fit into theirs. This is truly up to us to decide.

If we are willing to be embarrassed in front of people, we will learn the strength to overcome. If we are afraid to look ignorant to people, we may never ask the question that might be a breakthrough. Which is more stupid, not asking the question because we may be embarrassed, or never knowing the answer?

We can turn those stupid questions into our advantage, by understanding how the answer was given. If we are ridiculed for asking a question, then we know what type of person we are dealing with, and this is truly an advantage. Remember, that some dysfunctional people get their value by making us feel demeaned. This is getting the answer, and turning a disadvantage into advantage.

It can be seen as using our perceived weakness as an advantage. If we are ignorant, then asking questions will give us the information we desire to stop being ignorant. This is the test that everyone must pass willingly to surpass the ego-esteem. The ego-esteem is the obstacle to all things that are great. The ego-esteem is the barrier to one's own self-realization. The ego-esteem holds us back from experiencing everything that is hard to accomplish, because we are afraid to fail, so we won't try.

FREEDOM

This is the old catch twenty-two, the ego-esteem wants to be great, but the ego-esteem can't be shown up. Since the ego-esteem can't stand to be embarrassed, we can't give a one hundred percent effort, because the ego-esteem is afraid of losing, so we hold back and in holding back, we can't obtain the thing that might make us better, and not obtaining greatness is really just the fear of our ego-esteem.

We should always challenge ourselves to reach as high as we can, because only by failure and perseverance will we understand just who we are, and ignite our will to succeed. Are we willing to accept that our best may not be good enough? Remember, we are just not capable of competing at everyone's level, so are we willing to find this out? When it comes right down to it, do we want to find out the truth of who we are, or live in our own fantasy world? The person willing to find their truth is a real champion, because the true strength of the world is knowing reality.

True strength comes from not living in delusion, because it comes with it's costs and it will always let us down. This is turning disadvantage into advantage by knowing our limits and what is really going on, so we don't over step our abilities. A world-class golfer may never be a great ice skater, but if she wants to try and find out how far she can go, she is exploring her abilities. If it brings her joy in the effort, then it's the attempt that is important, which brings her closer to knowing herself.

Knowing our limitations is the truest test against the ego-esteem, by turning disadvantage into advantage. How many times have our decisions in life been based on ego-esteem, fear, expectations or dysfunction? How can we find happiness when we let our trivial, petty self decide for us? We find true happiness and peace by finding our true self, our real self.

FIND YOUR WAY

Truly be in charge of your own path, don't be driven by subconscious desires and motivations. We have to realize that all this is for us, and not for anyone else. It's a decision that must be made by each individual person, since no one has the right to control how other people act. Kill the ego esteem and find yourself.

If we realize the significance of the consequence of the desire of our ego on the people around us, we then realize that the world has to sacrifice for our own individual ego. To have no agenda for giving is to truly learn charity. To have no itinerary for the human race is learning real compassion. To love one another without being judgmental is to learn the importance of all individuals. Learning these things teaches us the true significance of consequence.

www.ingramcontent.com/pod-product-compliance
Lightning Source LLC
LaVergne TN
LVHW011426080426
835512LV00005B/281